IRELAND

A Photographic Journey

TEXT: **Terence Sheehy**

CAPTIONS: **Pauline Graham**

DESIGNED BY: **Teddy Hartshorn**

EDITORIAL: **Gill Waugh and Pauline Graham**

PRODUCTION: **Ruth Arthur and David Proffit**

DIRECTOR OF PRODUCTION: **Gerald Hughes**

DIRECTOR OF PUBLISHING: **David Gibbon**

CLB 2454
© 1990 Colour Library Books Ltd., Godalming, Surrey, England.
All rights reserved.
This 1990 edition published by Crescent Books,
distributed by Outlet Book Company, Inc., a Random House Company,
225 Park Avenue South, New York, New York 10003.
Printed and bound in Hong Kong.
ISBN 0 517 01500 5
8 7 6 5 4 3 2 1

IRELAND

A Photographic Journey

Text by
TERENCE SHEEHY

CRESCENT BOOKS
NEW YORK

The great paradox of Irish history is that because of it there are more Irishmen and Irishwomen living in the United States of America, in Canada, in Australia, in New Zealand, in South America and in Great Britain, than there are living in the Emerald Isle today.

The historian, Lord Macaulay, wrote of the Irish Diaspora, "there were Irish of great ability, energy, and ambition, but they were to be found everywhere except in Ireland: at Versailles, and at St. Ildefonso, in the armies of Frederick and in the armies of Maria Teresa. One exile became a marshal of France, another became Prime Minister of Spain. If he had stayed in his native land he would have been regarded as an inferior by all the ignorant and worthless squireens who drank the glorious and immortal memory. In his palace at Madrid he had the pleasure of being assiduously courted by the Ambassador of George II, and of bidding defiance to the Ambassador of George III. Scattered over all Europe were to be found brave Irish generals, dexterous Irish diplomatists, Irish counts, Irish barons, Irish Knights of St. Louis and of St. Leopold, of the White Eagle and of the Golden Fleece, who, if they had remained in the house of bondage, could not have been ensigns of marching regiments, or freemen of petty corporations."

Lecky, in Volume II of his famous *History of England*, gives a fascinating list of Irishmen who attained ranks of dignity and honor in literally every kingdom of Europe:

"Abroad there was hardly a Catholic country where Irish exiles or their children might not be found in posts of dignity and honour. Lord Clare became Marshal of France. Browne, who was one of the very ablest Austrian generals, and who took a leading part in the first period of the Seven Years' War, was the son of Irish parents; and Maguire, Lacy, Nugent and O'Donnell were all prominent generals in the Austrian service during the same war. Another Browne, a cousin of the Austrian Commander, was Field Marshal in the Russian service and Governor of Riga. Peter Lacy, who also became a Russian Field Marshal, and who earned a reputation as one of the finest soldiers of his time, was of Irish birth .... Of the Dillons more than one obtained high rank in the French Army, and one became Archbishop of Toulouse. The brave, the impetuous Lally of Tollendal (his Irish name was O'Mullally), who served with such distinction at Dettingen and Fontenoy, and who for a time seriously threatened the English power in Hindustan, was son of a Galway gentleman and member of an old Milesian family. Among Spanish generals, the names of O'Mahoney, O'Donnell, O'Gara, O'Reilly, and O'Neil sufficiently attest their nationality, and an Irish Jacobite named Cammock was conspicuous among the admirals of Alberoni. Wall, who directed the Government of Spain with singular ability from 1754 to 1763,was an Irishman, if not by birth, at least by parentage. McGeoghegan was Chaplain of the Irish Brigade in the service of France. The physician to Sobieski, King of Poland, and the physician to Philip V of Spain, were both Irish; and an Irish naturalist, named Bowles, was active in reviving the mining industry of Spain in 1752.

In the diplomacy of the Continent Irish names are not unknown. Tyrconnel was French Ambassador at the court of Berlin. Wall, before he became chief minister of Spain, had represented that country at the court of London. Lacy was Spanish Ambassador at Stockholm, and O'Mahony at Vienna."

Of the success of his fellow countrymen abroad, even Dean Swift, that most cynical of political observers, was moved to write: "I cannot too highly esteem those gentlemen of Ireland, who, with all the disadvantages of being exiles and strangers, have been able to distinguish themselves in so many parts of Europe, by their valour and conduct, above all other nations."

Surely some of the most prophetic words concerning Ireland and her people were written by Thomas Davis, the Poet of *The Nation*, in the concluding lines of his poem *The Battle Eve of the Brigade*, about the "Wild Geese" fighting for Louis of France, under the command of Count Thomond:

"For in far foreign fields, from Dunkirk to Belgrade,
  Lie the soldiers and chiefs of The Irish Brigade."

The Irish and America

The American connection is based on such enormous numbers of Irish men and women making their way to the New World for so many different reasons that nobody is quite sure of the actual numbers involved. It is estimated that in the period between 1717 and 1775 something like a quarter of a million Ulstermen settled in the North American continent and, between 1820 and 1920, something like four-and-a-quarter million people emigrated from Ireland to earn a living in the United States. The reasons for going were many.

The Ulster folk who emigrated did so voluntarily, and were almost entirely of Presbyterian stock, seeking to escape from the Protestant Ascendancy, with which they had little or nothing in common. The early Irish from the South were often bondsmen, who had sold their services as laborers, in advance of their emigrating. The millions who went on the move went because of the famines in Ireland. They crossed the Atlantic in fearful conditions and they died in their thousands of cholera on arrival. They came in the "coffin" ships from Queenstown, from Galway and from Liverpool. They were mainly from the hardest stricken areas of the western seaboard, from Clare, Mayo, Donegal, Kerry and Cork. They were unskilled laborers who tended to herd into the cities of the east coast, and they were the men who built the railroads of America and, in the main, were the hewers of wood and drawers of water.

Their Presbyterian brethren, who were the first emigrants, were the frontiersmen of the new America, and they brought their teachers and preachers with them to form comparatively well-educated and closely knit communities. Because they had suffered civil and religious restrictions at the hands of the Establishment in Ireland, the hardy Ulster Presbyterian folk found the United States a haven of freedom – for themselves, their Puritan neighbors and their Catholic compatriots. They were aptly described by President Roosevelt as "a grim, stern people, strong and simple, powerful for good and evil, swayed by gusts of stormy passion, the love of freedom rooted in their heart's core." Like all the white settlers of the time, however, their religious compassion did not include the native Red Indian, who was there to be massacred.

The alternatives for the log-cabin Irish were, all too frequently, kill or be killed. They more than survived – they prospered. They made, in many cases, vast fortunes, they gave America at least ten Presidents, if not a round dozen, and southern Ireland ultimately produced John F. Kennedy and Ronald Reagan. The round dozen would include Richard Nixon who, on his visit to Ireland, unearthed Irish ancestors on his Milhous side, and Jimmy Carter, who can claim Irish blood from the North of Ireland on his maternal side.

The Presidents from the historic counties of Ulster include Andrew Jackson, James Knox Polk, James Buchanan, Andrew Johnston, Ulysses Grant, Chester Arthur, Grover Cleveland, Benjamin Harrison, William McKinley and Woodrow Wilson. Three of them were born in Ulster, while the remainder were of Irish descent.

Andrew Jackson, President from 1829 to 1837, was the first American frontiersman President born in a log cabin. His father, a small tenant farmer near Carrickfergus in the county of Antrim, had married Elizabeth Hutchinson from the same county. They settled in the wilds of North Carolina, and Andrew, as a youth of thirteen, encountered the sword of a British dragoon in 1780. He suffered a cut to the bone in one arm, and was scarred on his head for life because, it is said, he refused to clean the officer's boots! He earned the title "Old Hickory" from his troops, who thought him as tough as the proverbial old hickory during the war of 1812 against the Creek Indians in Alabama. A lawyer and a soldier, he was a man of iron will.

James K. Polk, President from 1845 to 1849, was said to have been "the least conspicuous man who had ever been nominated for President." His ancestors came from Londonderry. He himself was born in North Carolina, and was a supporter of Andrew Jackson.

James Buchanan, the only bachelor President, held office from 1857 to 1861. He was the son of the Buchanans from Omagh, in the county of Tyrone, who emigrated to Pennsylvania. Known as "Old Buck," he was an extremely wealthy and successful lawyer.

Andrew Johnston was President from 1865 to 1869. A "poor white," born in poverty in North Carolina, he came of County Antrim stock, although little is known about his Irish antecedents.

Ulysses Grant, twice elected to the presidency between 1869 and 1877, was a leader of the Federal forces in the American Civil War. His mother, Hannah Simpson, came from Dungannon, in the county of Tyrone.

A friend and supporter of Grant, Chester A. Arthur was President from 1881 to 1885. His ancestors came from the village of Dreen in the county of Antrim and his grandfather emigrated to America in 1816, with his son, who became a Baptist preacher in Vermont, where Arthur was born.

Grover Cleveland, President from 1885 to 1889, was elected for a second term of office from 1893 to 1897. His Irish connection was on his mother's side as she was a Neal from County Antrim. He was, incidentally, one of the only Irish politicians to oppose the Tammany Hall machine of the New York Democratic Party – and to succeed.

Benjamin Harrison, a lawyer from Ohio, was President from 1889 to 1893. He was descended, on his mother's side, from the Northern Irish Irwin family.

William McKinley was President from 1897 to 1901. A kindly gentleman, he was the great-great-grandson of James McKinley, who emigrated to America in the mid 1700s, and came from Ballymoney, County Antrim. Like John F. Kennedy, William McKinley died at the hands of an assassin, who shot him down in cold blood on September 6th, 1901, in Buffalo.

Woodrow Wilson's ancestors hailed from Dergalt, near Strabane, in the county of Tyrone. President of the United States from 1913 to 1921, he was also President of the University of Princeton.

In contrast to all the Presidents with antecedents in the historic province of Ulster, the great-grandfather of President John F. Kennedy was born in the historic province of Leinster in the county of Wexford, in a cottage in Dunganstown, four miles from the town of New Ross. Here there is a John F. Kennedy memorial park and arboretum opened to his memory in 1968 by President de Valera.

The visit of John F. Kennedy to Ireland in 1963 gave the Irish people tremendous joy and satisfaction, as it was the first time an American President of Irish stock had taken the time to pay an official and very personal visit. His visit was a triumph, and in four short days he received the warmest and most genuine welcome ever given to a returning Irish-American. Five months later a weeping Ireland heard the tragic news from Dallas, Texas.

To commemorate the men who helped to expand the frontiers of America from 1717 onwards, the wealthy banking and industrial tycoons of Pittsburg, the Mellon family, have most generously set up an Ulster-American Folk Park in Camphill in the county of Tyrone. Dr. Mathew T. Mellon made the Folk Park possible and his family, of traditional Presbyterian stock, has re-created how the early frontiers people lived in the New World. Judge Thomas Mellon, the founding father of the Mellon fortune, was born at Camphill, and the Folk Park shows how the early settlers based their cabins and their schools and their place of worship on their village back home in the old country.

It is no small wonder that, since 250,000 Ulstermen are estimated to have emigrated to America between 1717 and 1775, there were at least eight signatories to the Declaration of Independence on July 4,1776, from Ireland.

The whole world resounds with the truth of their words: "We hold these truths to be self-evident, that all men are created equal, that they are endowed by the Creator with certain inalienable rights; that among these are life, liberty and the pursuit of happiness."

Irish signatories included James Smith, born in Dublin, Mathew Thornton from Limerick, who had left Ireland as a small boy, and George Taylor, a native Irishman. Edward Rutledge's family came from County Tyrone, and Charles Carroll, another signatory, was a grandson of an O'Carroll from the County of Offaly. Thomas Lynch was from a west of Ireland family, and Charles Thomson, who helped draft the Declaration of Independence, was originally from Dublin.

The Declaration itself was printed by John Dunlap, from Strabane in the County of Tyrone, and you can see today the shop in which he learnt his craft as a printer, Gray's Printing Shop in Strabane.

George Washington was surrounded by Irish officers, and two of his Irish generals were Richard Montgomery, who was killed in the attack on Quebec in 1775, and Richard Irvine, who commanded the Pennsylvania Regiment.

John Shee was another Irish general who commanded Irish volunteers from Pennsylvania, and Captain Jack Barry, born in Tacumshane in the county of Wexford, rose to be Commodore and earned his title, "the father of the American Navy." Washington's own secretary was James McHenry from Ballymena in the county of Antrim.

Accustomed as we are to hearing of the Irish Americans in the East coast cities of Boston, New York and Philadelphia, and in the midwest in Chicago, we are apt to forget that they flourished south of the Mason and Dixon line. Sam Houston, the first President of the Lone Star State, was of the Houston family of Ballynure in the county of Antrim. Daniel Boone, the first man to explore Kentucky, was Daniel "Buhun" of Irish stock. Davy Crockett, "King of the Wild Frontier," was the son of an emigrant from Londonderry. It was the Irish regiments from Pennsylvania, Maryland, Virginia and Kentucky who fought so magnificently in the campaigns of 1812.

The burning of the White House in 1814 was an extraordinary business. Both Colonel Arthur Brooke from the county of Fermanagh and Major General John Ross from Rostrevor, County Down, took leading parts in this affair, which was the culmination of raiding, pillaging and burning all along the coast of the United States. The prize money was good, and the captured tons of tobacco fetched top prices in Bermuda.

The peculiar officer status of the time meant that Ross could personally take a hand in setting fire to the Oval Room, while he had a number of veteran soldiers flogged for minor looting offences. The most shocking piece of sacrilege by the redcoats in the burning of the Capitol was the deliberate consignment to the flames of the hundreds of beautiful volumes purchased in Europe to found the American Library of Congress. Ross was to get his just deserts, as he was picked off by an American sharpshooter in the advance on Baltimore. He fell from his horse, and died of his wounds in a jolting farm cart,

which had been commandeered to take him out of the battle. As he lay dying, he sent for Colonel Brooke to take over supreme command. Brooke and his crack regiments of veteran redcoats were defeated in the final battle of the War of 1812. They and the British Navy were seen off the premises by the ploughboys of the volunteer militia of the army of the Young Republic, "by the dawn's early light."

All the world knows how Washington won the battle of Yorktown in the month of October, 1781, and how, at the surrender of the British general, Cornwallis, the British troops marched out led by a General O'Hara, who, with Irish gallantry, took the place of Cornwallis, who was too ill to move.

Speaking of Irish gallantry on the American scene, perhaps it is best to draw the veil quickly over the activities of the Costelloes and the O'Bannions, the Malones and the Sheehys in the bootlegging days of Prohibition. When apprehended, they all claimed in court that they were "as white as driven snow," for they were doing their thirsting neighbors a good turn, based on the days long ago back home when their ancestors had made "poteen" and distributed it throughout the neighboring countryside, without thought of profit.

A lovable, hospitable and hardworking section of the ethnic groups that go to make up the peoples of the United States, the Irish have always and will always retain a deep love for the land of their forebears.

For them, new life began under the Statue of Liberty, whose significant inscription appealed to the Celtic imagination –

"Keep, ancient lands, your storied pomp.
Give me your tired, your poor,
Your huddled masses yearning to breathe free,
The wretched refuse of your teeming shore,
Send these, the homeless tempest-tost to me,
I lift my lamp beside the golden door."

Ballyporeen, a village of several hundred inhabitants in southwest Tipperary, just eleven miles by the signpost in the square from Mitchelstown, produced two famous sons, one being Pat O'Brien, the affable veteran Hollywood film actor, and the other, the late Jack O'Brien, Batchelor of Arts, and first chief executive of the Irish Tourist Board. A brilliant man, he took a leading part in the War of Independence, and was a founding father of the Irish Tourist Board, now recognized as one of the most successful tourist boards in the world.

Ballyporeen used to be known as O'Farrell and O'Brien country, but recently it has become universally acknowledged as O'Reagan country – the ancestral home of Ronald Reagan, fortieth President of the United States of America. His ancestors came from the several hundred acres of bogland known as "Doolis," the Irish for "The Dark Fairy Place." At the turn of the eighteenth century, before the famines drove them away, some forty families lived there in their modest thatched cabins. Nothing now remains to mark any former human habitation. Debrett, the world authority on genealogy, has traced the Reagan family tree and suggested that the Regans – now spelt "Reagan"– were descended from Riagan, the nephew of Brian Boru, High King of Ireland, who defeated the Norsemen at the Battle of Clontarf in 1014.

The Doolis, where Reagan's ancestors were born, is a typical example of why hundreds of thousands of Irish folk left their native land for England, America and Canada. Fortunately, the townland of Doolis in the parish of Ballyporeen, and the surrounding countryside, is described in considerable detail by the journalist William O'Brien. O'Brien recorded his impressions in *The Freeman's Journal* in 1877, in a series of articles called *Christmas in the Galtees*. Before quoting the conditions which drove so many people from Ireland, including the Reagans, it is worth glancing at O'Brien's career.

He was born in Mallow, North Cork, in 1852, and died there in 1928. He worked on various newspapers and, like many nationalists, became a strong supporter of Charles Stewart Parnell. As a result of his powerful writing, he was jailed, with Parnell, in 1881. As a Member of Parliament for his native Mallow, he served under Parnell in the Irish Parliamentary Party. He is well remembered for organising a strike on the estate of Lord Kingston which resulted in the Mitchelstown "massacre," when the military forces of the Crown opened fire in the square, killing three people. O'Brien was arrested on a number of occasions and in 1890 fled to America for a while. During the 1890s, appalled by the hunger and misery of the people in Mayo, he agitated on their behalf. The following passage, taken from *Christmas in the Galtees* illustrates that misery:

"As I returned to Mitchelstown today after completing some inquiries respecting a neighbouring estate, a starved-looking and half-naked old woman, barefooted, and shivering with age and pain, besought me to see her cabin in a remote part of Doolis, where we had not been able to penetrate the previous night. Another tenant, David Russell of Doolis, who has also been served with an eviction order, volunteered to pilot me across the bogs. I followed into a shaking morass across which there is a precarious avenue of stepping stones, surrounded by filthy quagmires stocked with snipe. In his anxiety to allow me to use the dry places, my pioneer went almost to his knees in water. He did not seem to think this remarkable.

"At last we came to the cabin. It may have been because it was the last I saw, but the impression of horror and sickness left upon my mind by the sight of it fills me with loathing even while I write.

"The unfortunate creature had built it herself of sods and stones, and thatched it with heather and rushes. The approaches to it were swimming with liquid manure and mud; the odours around the place were revolting. Heaps of stones and bits of timber were fastened against the walls here and there to prevent them from falling to pieces. Inside all was darkness.

"My companion took the door off its one hinge to give light. It was even more shocking to see than to imagine what was there; not a gleam of fire in the hearth, neither dressing table nor box; the window was filled with stones to keep out the storm; a coarse platter of yellow stirabout without even salt, represented the whole food of the establishment, and an iron pot the entire furniture. There were stones for seats, a mound of flags for a bedstead. Inside the door was a heap of stones as a rude buttress to support the crumbling wall.

"In this desolate rookery the Widow Condon spent Christmas night, having begged a meal of bread and tea from her neighbours as her Christmas dinner. Her holding is one swampy field upon which the rent has been raised from 2/6 to 25/-. She spent 30/- for manure and 10/- for labour in an attempt to grow a quarter of an acre of potatoes, but it produced not a stone of potatoes. She hasn't a cow, sheep or even a hen. She pawned her clothes to pay the last half of the revised rent and is indebted to neighbours for the castaway clothing she wears.

"As I drove away this evening to Cahir, past Lord Lismore's ample demesne, past the rich expanses of luxuriant grass and deep corn lands, ploughed for spring sowing, past orchards and barns and bursting farmyards and the trim rows of model cottages which border the Lady Charteris' Park walls, it was hard to think that I still breathed the air of the same county which enclosed all the barrenness and blight and all the suffering and sorrow I left behind me around the Galtees."

Small wonder that the Reagan family had left all this some thirty years before. Ronald Reagan's great-grandfather was baptized Michael O'Regan in the church of Ballyporeen on September 3rd, 1829. He was a son of Thomas O'Regan, laborer, of the parish of Ballyporeen in the townland of Doolis, who had married Margaret Murphy in 1817, and who was dead by the 1850s. Thomas had other children: Nicholas, who emigrated to Fairhaven, Illinois, and daughters Elena, Margaret and Elizabeth. Michael emigrated to England in famine times and on October 31st, 1852 he married Catherine Mulcahy. His occupation was described as "Laborer." His brother Nicholas signed as a witness with an "X." It is possible that the O'Regans and Regans were Irish speaking, and not literate in English which would explain the spelling of their name in the parish register as "Reagan." They were among thousands of emigrants who lost the "O" or the "Mac" to their names, or had their Irish names misspelt in English. Like many of their countrymen, the Reagans settled in South London, and Michael worked as a soapmaker. On May 29th, 1854, Ronald Reagan's grandfather John was born, and the Reagans emigrated in 1858 to Illinois, via Canada, where the parents worked on the farmlands and owned considerable property. John married a lady of Irish descent, who had been born in Canada, and the youngest of their three children, John Reagan, became the father of the President. The rest is modern history.

History, in Irish terms, is still being made, and Reagan was the very first American President to visit the Irish Embassy in Washington when he celebrated

Saint Patrick's Day there at a luncheon on March 17th, 1981. The lunch, in his honor, was given by His Excellency Mr Sean Donlon, the Irish Ambassador, and Mrs Donlon. Other distinguished American guests of Irish ancestry were the Speaker of the House of Representatives, Mr 'Tip' O'Neill, Secretary of the Treasury, Mr Regan, and Senator Edward Kennedy. To commemorate the day, the President was presented with a genealogical chart tracing his ancestors back to Ballyporeen in County Tipperary. He also received a St. Patrick's Day gift of shamrock in a Beleek china basket, and was presented with an Irish silver dish for his wife, Nancy. The children of the Irish Ambassador to the United States were presented, by the President, with a Waterford glass bowl full of green jellybeans, the President's favorite conference table sweet.

On the same St. Patrick's Day, various American political leaders, in a special Feast Day message, formed the "Friends of Ireland." The announcement was initially signed by no less than eleven senators, ten Congressmen and the Governors of three states! The Irish are world famous for possessing the "gift of the gab," an ability which is upheld by various Irish societies and institutions. One society in particular, the Eire Society of Boston, reserves awards for what it considers remarkable achievements. For example, in 1954, it awarded its annual gold medal to "a person who has rendered outstanding services in furthering the purpose of the Society" – Michael Houlihan – who was described by the Society as follows:

"Priest, historian, writer, orator. He utilized a variety of media – the pulpit, the speaker's rostrum, the motion picture, the printed word, the classroom – to interpret the soul of Ireland, and Ireland's culture to an American audience that has been charmed by his gracious wit, edified by his erudition, and inspired by the superior quality of his message.

"He has been a veritable treasurer of Irish lore, collecting a scholar's library of Irish literature, drama, history, archaeology, and genealogy that will one day form a striking and significant addition to the library resources of this area. He has sought unceasingly by personal travel, research and investigation, to wrest from the reluctant soil of New England the history of the early Irish immigrants to these shores.

"His life has been motivated by the desire to pass on to others this great treasury of Irish lore. In the parish school and high school, in the organizations to which he has given counsel and encouragement, and in the larger audience which he has so successfully reached, the results of his labors have been evidenced by a wider awareness and deeper appreciation of Irish culture and scholarship.

"The Eire Society pays tribute to this accomplishment which reflects so ably the purposes for which this Society was founded."

Houlihan's reply reflects his emotions at being thus honored:

"... I am deeply moved by the honor that the Eire Society of Boston has done me by giving me the Gold Medal for 1954. It is difficult to put words together to express adequately the profound emotions that well up in my heart. Recognition by this honorable Society every year of someone who has rendered outstanding service in furthering its purposes, has come to be an event of, shall I say, national note. And to select one of its own members is most heartening indeed. But this year's choice makes me quite sure that the prerogative of infallibility has not yet been vouchsafed to the Society's councils.

"But, seriously, my feelings tonight are all mixed up. Naturally, I am proud – proud of the honor. Pride comes by me easily. The very root-source of my surname means 'proud' in the Gaelic. And who will say that pride is not betimes a virtue! Even though it has from time to time wrought havoc since before Paradise. Who will question St. Paul's virtue when he boasted '*Civis Romanus sum*' (I am a Roman Citizen), or when he prided himself as a native of Tarsus – 'no mean city.' And I have a great pride, too, in that my surname is part of one of the symbolic names of Ireland, Cathleen Ni Houlihan. And so my pride tonight comes to the top in having this great honor conferred on me.

"But mine is also a feeling of lowliness. I have said it is most heartening to have the Society recognize one of its own members. But within that same membership could be easily and readily selected many a one who has rendered more outstanding service to the ideals of our group. I feel like Maude Gonne McBride who tells of her vision of the fair Cathleen, back over the years of her life. She writes 'It was then that I saw her, Cathleen Ni Houlihan in all her beauty, her dark hair blowing in the wind, going toward the hills, springing from stone to stone, over the treacherous surface of the bog. The gleaming white stones before her marked her path and faded into the darkness. I heard a voice say "you are one of those little stones on which the feet of the Queen rest a moment on her way to freedom." Then the sadness of the night and loneliness overwhelmed me and I wept. Now old and not triumphant, I know the blessedness of having been one of those little stones on the path to freedom.'

"Yes, the 'little stones' on which the feet of Cathleen have rested disappear in the dark loneliness of night. It is blessed to have been for a moment one of these little stones.

"But, my good friends, my strongest feeling tonight is not one of pride or lowliness. Rather, it is one of prayer. Prayer, as you know, has four great ends, four outlets of expression. These we find in the great Christian Sacrifice of the Cross and of the Holy Mass, and as equally in the Christ-giving simple 'Our Father.' They are the expression of love and adoration, of thanksgiving, of expiation and of petition. These are the feelings that surge up in my heart, tonight, in a kind of wildness and fury.

"Mine is a feeling of adoration and love, primarily, of course, to God Almighty, who as God of all nations, has given me Ireland to love and cherish, a veritable bit of heaven from out of the sky.

'He made you all fair,
You, in purple and gold,
You, in silver and gold,
Till no eye that has seen,
Without love, can behold.'

"Mine is a feeling of thanksgiving. Thanksgiving to God and to you, indeed, for what has been given me this night. Thanks to the great God that gave us Ireland as our Motherland. Thanks for the blood in my veins that comes down from the days of the Red Branch and the Fianna – 'down the ringing grooves' of time. Thanks for the countless glories and sufferings, vouchsafed to that Motherland – glories galore, and the shiningest of all, her stalwart faith, bequeathed to her by the saintly son of Succat – and sufferings galore that were the very test of her faith, that faith that makes you and me today both Christian and Catholic. Thanks, too, for the *'felix culpa'* 'the happy fault', the forced mass immigration of her children to these shores, the *'sine qua non'* that makes it possible for me to boast 'I am an American Citizen.' *'Civis Romanus sum'* said St. Paul. *'Civis Americanus sum'* say we all profoundly and with thanks to the God who loves the Irish and thanks to the Irish who love God.

"And mine is a feeling of expiation, in that I have been priviliged to share with you all in the sufferings and persecutions of the Irish race, not the least of which was that of being unknown and misunderstood, sufferings that helped to 'fill up what was wanting' in those of Christ, sufferings that are a part of the great atonement so ably contributed to by the patience, endurance and long-sufferance of the Irish race. If I have shared with the Eire Society of Boston in expiation and atonement for the past, it was to ensure the success of your great objective, the spread of a wider and deeper appreciation of Irish culture and scholarship.

"And finally, mine is a feeling of petition to the throne of God, on behalf of the Eire Society and of Mother Ireland.

"For the Eire Society: yours is an honorable commission. It is not unlike that of the Savior to His apostles. It is a commission to 'go forth.' Go forth and preach the gospel, the good news of Irish culture, among all peoples, in the byways and highways. Go forth and spread the news, spread the awareness among your own and those who are not your own. And my prayer is that God give you the lift to do that same, that, as Patrick planted, you may be given the grace to water and God will give the increase.

"And a prayer for Ireland: may the day be not far off when she takes her rightful place in the sun. And may we be granted the boon and benison to live to see that day, when maybe some stranger from Piccadilly will come up to us and say: 'Did you see an old woman going down the path?' And we may answer,
'No. I did not. But I saw a young girl, and she had the walk of a Queen.'"

At the same dinner of the Eire Society of Boston, one of the guests of honor was the world renowned film director, John Ford. An American, both proud of his country, and of his Irish origins, John Ford's father, Sean O'Fearna (his real name), came from Spiddal in County Galway – an Irish speaking district – and his mother, Barbara Curran, was a native Irish speaker from the Aran Islands. John "Ford" was born in the state of Maine, graduated from Portland High School, Oregon (a state to which his parents had moved), and studied later at the University of Maine. He learnt his trade the hard way in motion pictures, beginning his career in 1917, and specializing in Westerns. By 1924, he had made his name with his now well-known silent motion picture *The Iron Horse*, a Western epic about the laying of the first American railway tracks.

Like many men of Irish ancestry, John Ford enjoyed horse racing, and his first romantic Irish film, made in 1926, was called *Shamrock Handicap*. *Mother Machree*, starring Victor McLaglen, followed in 1928, and *Hangman's House*, an Irish drama-comedy, later that year. Classics in "talkies" now began to appear, such as *The Lost Patrol* in 1934, whose cast included the Abbey Theater actor J.M. Kerrigan.

In 1935 came Ford's great film *The Informer*, based on the novel by a writer from the Aran Islands, Liam O'Flaherty. This film featured a host of Irish actors such as J.M. Kerrigan, Denis O'Dea, Leo McCabe and Una O'Connor. *The Informer* won an Academy Award. It was based on the Dublin of "the Trouble," a Dublin of the Black and Tans, and trench-coated IRA men. Filmed in three weeks, and made on a shoestring budget, it had psychological implications and was far in advance of its time, with all the symbolism and power of a great classic tragedy. Strangely enough it had strong overtones of James Joyce, and silences, as well as music, were used in a highly novel and experimental way. *The Informer* established John Ford as a director of world renown.

In 1937, Ford directed Sean O'Casey's play, *The Plough and the Stars*, and with this film the Abbey actors arrived in force on the Hollywood scene. They included Barry Fitzgerald, Dennis O'Dea, Eileen Crowe, F.J. McCormick – probably the greatest Abbey actor of all time – Una O'Connor and Arthur Shields (Barry Fitzgerald's brother).

Another Academy Award winner, *Stagecoach*, came out in 1939, and in 1940 both *The Grapes of Wrath* by Steinbeck and *The Long Voyage Home* by Eugene O'Neill were released.

Somehow, even in his Westerns, Ford found room to add touches of Irish tradition – in one film for example, for no apparent reason, a group of frontier U.S. cavalry men are seen, and heard, singing "The Bold Fenian Men!" Ford manages to slip hints of his Irish heritage into his films, both for his own amusement and for the sake of the country of his ancestors.

His Irishness was truly imprinted upon the history of Hollywood when he filmed *The Quiet Man*, a beautiful color film which captured the rapturous scenery of County Galway and County Mayo, and put Ireland on the 1950s' tourist map.

When *The Quiet Man* came out, the late Paddy Purcell thought that the film was based on his novel of the same title. However, it transpired that the title was also the title of a short story, written for a popular American magazine, by Maurice Walsh.

With the development of this short story, Ford had made a moving picture which put Ireland well and truly on the scenic map of the world. While the film was being made in the west of Ireland in 1951, the cast stayed in Ireland's most famous castle hotel, Ashford Castle, near the village of Cong, in County Mayo, formerly the country seat of the Guinness family. It was then run by one of Ireland's best hoteliers, Noel Huggard. Huggard had learnt his trade in the family hotel in Waterville, County Kerry. He played host to many famous actors, including John Wayne, Maureen O'Hara, Victor McLaglen and Barry Fitzgerald. Ten weeks of filming and Ireland appeared on the world's screens as a place of incomparable greens and blues, and incredible beauty. The genuine scenery was so breathtakingly beautiful that the plot of the film, which was light and full of every Irish cliché, hardly mattered. And yet John Ford, though fully immersed in the landscape and people of his mother from the Aran Islands and his father from Spiddal, knew precisely what he was portraying. Millions of Irish both in America and throughout the world loved it, and flocked to Ireland as tourists to see for themselves. Even the Irish in Ireland loved it, in spite of Maureen O'Hara being "dragged by the black roots of her red hair" through the fields by John Wayne, as a film critic so succinctly put it.

The plot of the film was almost over-simple. John Wayne portrays Sean Thorton, a returned Yankee in search of his family homestead. Traditional matchmaking – the arranged Irish marriage – is a further cliché, and, of course, there has to be the mother and father of all clichés, the fight across the fields between Red Will Danaher, brother of Red Head Kate – Maureen O'Hara – and former American champion boxer, Sean Thorton. The landscape of Ireland is the real star of the film, and John Ford, with enormous artistry, captures the immense beauty of his motherland.

This very simple romantic story, which could have been an enormous sentimental flop, succeeded because Maurice Walsh, the Irish romantic novelist, was in the John Buchan class, and knew his people – and the plain people of Ireland were portrayed by world renowned actors.

John Ford was greatly assisted and influenced in his filming in Ireland by his friendship with people such as Michael, Lord Killanin of Galway, a journalist of note and sensitivity, by Noel Huggard and by a host of other friends who were only too happy to see their country so favorably and expertly portrayed on the world's screens. *The Quiet Man* had the unique distinction of pleasing two worlds, that of the Irish-American, two thousand miles away, with the love light of the Lake Isle of Innisfree still in his eyes, and also the world of the people of Ireland, who were amused and entertained, and who also had the prospect of silver dollars and pounds sterling reflected in their smiling Irish eyes!

The Irish, in this instance, were lucky, for Hollywood was quite capable, and still is, of producing the most appalling and laughable bilge about the Emerald Isle. One classic example was the 1937 Metro-Goldwyn-Mayer production of *Parnell*, which featured none other than Clark Gable as Parnell, and Myrna Loy as Kitty O'Shea. Getting history entirely wrong – a Hollywood hazard – the director and producer, John M. Stahl, had John Steward Parnell-Gable promising, on his death bed, to marry Myrna Loy-Kitty O'Shea !

Hollywood of the 'Thirties, under the vulgar control of the tycoons who ran M-G-M at the time, was able to reconstruct almost the entire British House of Commons for this drama, and threw in, for good measure, an "Irish village," made in California, inhabited by some fifteen hundred "Irish" extras who were stage-Irish to end all stage-Irish.

Such is the resilience of Hollywood that it was able to withstand this unsuccessful attempt at portraying the famous Parnell-Shea divorce case, and M-G-M. were content to write off their Irish village, and their House of Commons sets, and let the film quietly die.

The history books of Ireland, and those published in Europe, have very little to say of the real number of Irish emigrants who made their way to the United States. Lecky in his *History of England in the Eighteenth Century*, says: "Already, in 1775, the many disastrous circumstances of Irish history had driven great bodies of Irishmen to seek a home in America."

The very earliest Irish settlers were Irishmen such as the O'Carrolls, or Carrolls, who founded Maryland and Carrollstown in 1689. Charles Carroll of Carrollstown, who was born in 1737, was a signatory of the American Declaration of Independence. John Carroll became the first Catholic bishop. The America of the 1790s had a population of roughly three million people, and of these there were some 40,000 Irish born, while four times that number were of Irish descent. The Irish founded new towns in Massachusetts, such as Worcester, and the O'Sullivan family founded the town of Belfast in the state of Maine. In the 1730s, the Irish settled in Philadelphia in large numbers, and Irish emigrants helped to found Williamsburg and many small towns in Virginia.

By the 1820s, of the many millions pouring into the United States from Europe, nearly four million were Irish. With famine stalking the homeland in the hungry 'Forties, about two million starving peasants found their way to the hospitable shores of America, and by the 1850s the figures had leapt from thirty thousand a year to several hundred thousand! The displaced peasants of Ireland, strangely enough, did not head for the countryside and the rural life but fell upon the growing East Coast cities of New York, Boston, Philadelphia, and Baltimore. By the 1850s, of New York's population of half a million, more than one hundred thousand were either Irish born or of Irish descent.

While these were humble and hungry peasants, their great advantage over their European neighbors was that they were politically aware. They had seen and experienced the growth of the democratic process, and the political organisational ability of Daniel O'Connell, the "Liberator" lawyer from County Kerry. He had put to work a vast political machine of people to win Catholic Emancipation. In the same way, the Irish in America were able to organize themselves on a political basis. Even in the revolution, the American War of Independence, the Irish were to the fore, and the historian Lecky points out that half of Washington's army was made up of Irish regiments. At Yorktown too, three quarters of the forces were Irish, and, after the Declaration of Independence, a special service of thanksgiving was held by them in Philadelphia, on the 4th July, 1779, in the presence of the President, all the members of Congress, and the heads of both the Army and the Navy.

Once the wave upon wave of Irish emigrants had found work in America they began to send remittances home to Ireland, and, of course, to encourage their relations to follow in their footsteps. The Irish laborers of the 1840s sent about a million dollars back to their homeland, and by the 1870s, when more than ten million dollars was flowing back to Ireland, the country's dependence on the "Letter from America" became not only a way of life, but a means of existence, particularly in the congested districts of the west coast counties of Ireland.

By the turn of the century, the Irish had settled in as part of the labor force, working from dawn to dusk, often in appallingly bad conditions generated by New World capitalist cities. They were shopkeepers, saloon keepers, gamblers, prize-fighters, and railroad gangers. They were, in the main, the pick-and-shovel brigade, who began to move west as the railroad tracks were laid. They were the builders of roads and houses, and diggers of gold and silver.

They began to fill San Francisco and Virginia City, and they were among the first to strike it rich in the new silver and gold mines of the West. Some who made it to Nob Hill became bankers and industrialists, and Nevada and Virginia City resounded with Irish names in the mid nineteenth century.

Not only were the Irish prominent members of the manual labor force, but they also took a high proportion of the editorial and reporting jobs in the emergent newspaper world. Men like Patrick Ford, from Galway, started their own papers such as *The Irish World*.

In the Civil War the Irish fought for both the Union Cause and for the cause of the Confederate Army. In New York alone the Irish contributed huge numbers to the colors, 50,000 fighting for the Union Army from the State of New York. The famous "Fighting 69th" regiment was formed and led by Colonel Michael Corcoran, and General Thomas Meagher, "Meagher of the Sword." Irish troops were prominent in the first and second battle of Bull Run, at Gettysburg, Fredericksburg and Antietan. They incurred severe losses, and had to be constantly replenished by fresh intakes of Irish troops. Of the Union forces, no less than thirty-eight regiments could be termed "Irish." "The Fighting 69th" took part

in World War I and continued its Irish-American heritage thereafter.

Probably one of the greatest contributions to the life of the United States by the Irish born, and those of Irish descent, lay in their natural talent for politics. In this field they were at a great advantage over their neighbors of other nationalities. They had a strong command of the English language, they had muscle, they had inherited the Daniel O'Connell political know-how, and in the cities they were organized in strongly knit parishes of families who all knew each other and inter-married to strengthen their bonds of kinship.

Tammany Hall, originally founded in 1789 and the leading political machine in New York, was taken over by the Irish in the 1850s – by orators, lawyers, journalists, saloonkeepers, teachers, police, firemen, and by small-time politicians.

In no time the Irish had produced men such as James Curley, born of Galway parents, and Mayor of Boston at the age of thirty five, and Al Smith, a precursor of John F. Kennedy, who obtained sixteen million votes in the election for the Presidency of the United States, and was only beaten because he was a Catholic, and not a prohibitionist. His story is best illustrated in the famous novel *The Last Hurrah*.

The "lace curtain" Irish soon arrived in Boston, New York and San Francisco. Success stories emerged, like that of William Grace, born in Cork, who built up the Grace Line, and had become a shipping millionaire in the late 1800s. The Irish had truly "arrived," in all walks of life in America, and as one Irish writer put it, writing in the 1920s, "There are Judges by the dozen, including a third of the Supreme Court, three Cardinals, Senators, multi-millionaires and captains of industry by the score, like Mr. Henry Ford, the motor king, Mr. Doheny who dominates the petrol industry, Mr. Thomas F. Ryan, the partner of King Leopold in the Congo diamond mines, Mr. Mellon, the secretary to the Treasury, Mr. Dougherty, the Attorney-General, Mr. Smith, the governor of New York, Mr. Hylan, the Mayor of New York, Mr. Tumulty, private secretary to President Wilson, General O'Ryan of the American Army, Dudly Malone, chief official of the port of New York, J.F. Ryan, the head of the Copper Trail, John Mitchel, Mayor of New York, Colonel Concanon, chairman of the White Star Line, and J.A. Farrell, President of the U.S. Steel Co."

The life of Richard "Boss" Croker of Tammany Hall gives an insight into the political power of the Irish in America. An Irish politician, he took over politics at local and then at national level.

Richard Croker was born in Ireland in 1841, in Clonakilty in the county of Tipperary. He came from a family of the Protestant faith who had settled in Ireland. He was brought to America, in 1846, by his father, Eyre Coote Croker. For the early part of his life in New York City he saw his father work as a veterinary surgeon for the horses on the city's tramcars. He had very little schooling, and worked as a prize fighter, and on the railroad, and in 1868 became an Alderman of Tammany Hall, entering into the rough and tumble of ward politics.

He became a city coroner, and in 1874 he was put on trial for murder for shooting a member of the opposition during the elections! The jury could not agree upon a verdict and, after some months in jail, he was set free. He graduated to fire chief, and then city chamberlain, and by 1889 he was leader of the Tammany Hall political machine. Within ten years or so of political life, having inside knowledge of city affairs, he had amassed a fortune, particularly from property speculations, making a million for almost each year of his leadership. He lived in considerable style on Fifth Avenue, and like all the millionaires of his day, he had his symbol of prestige – his own private railroad car. Tammany Hall ran New York, and Croker was able to retire from politics in 1903 and return to Ireland, after extensive travel in Europe. He maintained an expensive racing stud in Ireland, and he had the distinction of having his horse Orby win the English Derby, in 1907. He was over eighty when he died, leaving a fortune of millions of dollars to his widow.

The Glencairn Estate in Sandyford, County Dublin, now the residence of the British ambassador, was once Croker's property. The stables were taken over by Seamus McGrath, able son of Joe McGrath, founder of the Irish Hospitals' Trust Sweepstakes and of Waterford Glass. "Boss" Croker lies in Kilgobbin cemetery, and, if you look through the railings of part of his one-time estate, you will still see today a "gallop" laid out for his horse Orby, which is an exact replica of Tattenham Corner on the famous Epsom Downs race track. It is a left-hand, downhill turn which must have stood Orby in good stead when he faced the real thing at the Derby.

Mayor James Curley was one of the outstanding orators of his time. Much loved by the ordinary people of Boston, he was one of the first Irish Catholics to live in one of the lovely houses in the residential area favored by the Boston bourgeoisie. To mark the occasion, he had the wooden shutters of his house decorated with little shamrocks, hinting to his neighbors that the Irish had come into their own.

The Irish have certainly contributed their fair share to the world of literature – Eugene O'Neill, F. Scott Fitzgerald and John O'Hara are all of Irish ancestry.

Scott Fitzgerald displayed his Irish Romantic touch when he wrote lines such as the following on America, in his work *The Crack-Up*, on the relations between Europe and the U.S.A:

"France was a land, England was a people, but America, having about it still that quality of the idea, was harder to utter – it was the graves of Shiloh and the tired, drawn, nervous faces of its great men, and the country boys dying in the Argonne for a phrase that was empty before their bodies withered – it was a willingness of heart."

That "willingness of heart" has been shown by the Irish Americans who have been in the forefront of battles in six wars: the War of Independence, the Civil War, World War I, World War II, Korea, and Vietnam.

It is interesting to note that the Great Seal of the United States was designed by an Irishman, Charles Thompson who, as Secretary of State of the Congress, signed the Declaration of Independence in July, 1776. John Dunlap, who printed the original Declaration of Independence, was also the founder of the first daily newspaper in America, *The Pennsylvania Packet.*

Look at Leinster House in Dublin today, the seat of the Irish Parliament, and you will see that the White House in Washington was based on this former home of the Duke of Leinster, and it was designed by James Hoban, an architect who was born in County Carlow.

William Penn, founder of Pennsylvania, was born in Macroom, in County Cork. He was Clerk of the Admiralty Court in the harbor of Kinsale.

It was in Youghal, in County Cork, that Sir Walter Raleigh first smoked tobacco from America and grew the first potatoes from that country.

John Holland, born in Liscanllor, County Clare in 1841, invented the submarine, worked in the U.S. Navy and died in Newark, New Jersey in 1914.

The University town of Berkeley, in California, is named after Bishop George Berkeley of Cloyne, in County Cork, who was born in Thomastown in County Kilkenny in 1685. A philosopher of world standing, he spent three years in America.

The list of famous Irish-Americans is never ending and, in political life today, the affairs of Ireland are very much in the hearts and minds of the "Four Horsemen" – Mr 'Tip' O'Neill, Speaker of the House of Representatives, Senator Edward Kennedy, Senator Daniel Moynihan and former New York Governor, Hugh Carey. They are part of an Irish tradition that spans the time from the O'Carrolls of Maryland of 1689, to the Ronald Reagans of our time.

In the history of the Irish contribution to the United States of America, more is made of their contribution to the Northern States than that to those in the South. However, there is a truly magnificent piece of American rhetoric by the famous author and humorist, Irwin S. Cobb, taken from his address to a distinguished audience of the American Irish Historical Society in New York in 1917. Recalling his boyhood in the deep South, he said:

"As a boy, down south, there were two songs that stirred me as no other songs could – one was a song that I loved and one a song that I hated, and one of these songs was the battle hymn of the south, *Dixieland* and the other was *Marching Through Georgia*. But once upon a time when I was half-grown, a wandering piper came to the town where I lived, a man who spoke with a brogue and played with one. And he carried under his arm a weird contraption which to me seemed to be a compound of two fishing poles stuck in a hot-water bottle, and he snuggled it to his breast and it squawked out its ecstasy, and then he played on it a tune called *Garryowen*. And as he played it, I found that my toes tingled inside my shoes, and my heart throbbed as I thought it could only throb to the air of *Dixie*. And I took counsel with myself and I said, 'Why is it that I who call myself a pure Anglo-Saxon should be thrilled by an Irish air?' So I set out to determine the reason for it. And this is the kind of Anglo-Saxon I found out I was:

"My mother was of the strain, the breed of Black Douglas of Scotland, as Scotch as haggis, and rebels, all of them, descendants of men who followed the fortunes of Bonnie Prince Charles, and her mother lived in a county in North Carolina, one of five counties where, up to 1820, Gaelic was not only the language of the people in the street, but was the official language of the courts. It was in that same part of North Carolina that there lived some of the men who, nearly a year before our Declaration of Independence was drawn up, wrote and signed the Mecklenburg Declaration, which was the first battle-cry raised for American independence. On the other side, I found, by investigation, that my father's line ran back, straight and unbroken, to a thatched cottage on the green side of a hill in the Wicklow Mountains, and his people likewise had some kinsmen in Galway, and some in Dublin with whom, following the quaint custom of their land, they were accustomed to take tea and fight afterwards. I found I had a collateral ancestor who was out with the pikes in the '98 and he was taken prisoner and tried for high crimes and misdemeanors against the British Government, and was sentenced to be hanged by the neck until he was dead and might God have mercy on his soul! And he was hanged by the neck until he was dead, and I am sure God did have mercy on his soul, for that soul of his went marching on, transmitting to his people, of whom I am proud to be one, the desire to rebel against oppression and tyranny.

"I like to think of another Irishman, Mathew Lyon by name, the son of a humble Wicklow peasant, who was sold as a slave to the New England plantations because he, an Episcopalian, dared to raise his voice and his arm in defense of the rights of his Catholic neighbors and kinsmen in the County of Wicklow. He bought his freedom with a black bull which, according to family tradition, he first stole, and he became a United States Senator from Vermont, and cast the vote – against the wishes of his constituents – that made Thomas Jefferson President of this country over Aaron Burr, and by so doing altered the entire course of our country's history; and while he was in jail in a town in Vermont for his attacks on the odious alien and sedition laws, he issued a challenge for a duel to the President of the United States, and being released he moved to Kentucky and became a Congressman and later, having quarreled with all his neighbors there, he moved on to Arkansas and was named as Arkansas' first territorial delegate to Washington, and he might have moved still further west and might have filled still more offices had he not in the fullness of his maturity, when he was seventy years young, been thrown from a mule and had his neck broken."

Of the "Lost tribes of the Irish" in the South he said: "The state of Kentucky from which I hail has been called the cradle of the Anglo-Saxon race in America, and it has been said that the mountaineers of that state, with their feuds and their Elizabethan, Chaucerian methods of speech represent the purest strains of English blood to be found today on this continent. Now, then let us see

if that is true. I have looked into that matter and I tell you that fifty per cent, at least, of the dwellers of the mountains of the South, and notably of Kentucky and Virginia, are the lineal descendants of runaway indenture men, Irish rebels mainly, from the Virginian plantations. I know a mountain county in Kentucky of which half of the population bear one of three names. They are either Mayos, or Patricks, or Powers. And I once heard an orator stand up before an audience of those Mayos and Powers and Patricks and congratulate them on their pure English descent, and they believed it."

Discussing the earliest settlers in Kentucky he said: "The first man to explore Kentucky was an Irishman by the name of John Finley. But before him was still another Irish man by the name of McBride – James McBride. He lingers in state history as a shadowy figure, but I like to think of him as a red-haired chap with a rifle in one hand and possibly a demijohn in the other, coming out through the trackless wilderness alone and landing from his canoe on what was afterwards to be known as the Dark and Bloody ground. Aside from his name, it is proven that he was an Irishman by the legendary circumstances that immediately after coming ashore he carved his name in deep and enduring letters in the bark of the largest beech tree of the forest, and claimed all of the land that lay within his vision as his own, and shot an Indian or two and went on his way rejoicing. As for Daniel Boone, the great pathfinder, he really was descended from the line of Buhun, which is Norman-Irish and his mother was a Morgan, and his wife was a Bryan, and his father was an Irish Catholic."

He paid tribute to the wandering Irish schoolmasters who taught the children of the pioneers of Kentucky in their log cabins, so that eventually "Irishmen from Kentucky, Virginia, Pennsylvania and Maryland bore the brunt of the western campaigns in 1812 against the British. Irishmen from Kentucky fell thick at the disastrous battles of the Thames, and the Raison, and their Irish bones today rest in that ground, sanctifying it and making of it an American shrine of patriotism. It was the hand of a Kentucky Irishman, Colonel Richard Johnson, afterwards Vice-President of the United States, that slew the great Tecumseh. A good share of the Kentucky and Tennessee riflemen, who at New Orleans stood behind Andy Jackson's cotton bale breastworks, mowing down Packenhams Peninsular Veterans and making their red coats redder still with the life blood of those invaders, were Irishmen, real Irishmen. They proved their Irish lineage by the fact that they fell out and quarreled with Old Hickory because he denied them all the credit for winning the fight, and he quarreled back, for he was by way of being an Irishman himself."

Irwin Cobb went on to tell his audience of "... a Southern Irishman, the son of an Irish refugee, Pat Cleburne of Arkansas, one of the most gallant leaders that the Civil War produced. Pat Cleburne died on one of the bloodiest battlefields of Christendom in his stocking feet because as he rode into battle that morning he saw one of his Irish boys from Little Rock tramping barefooted over the frozen furrows of a wintry cornfield leaving tracks of blood behind him. So he drew off his boots and bade the soldier put them on, and fifteen minutes later he went to his God in his stocking feet. Raleigh laid down his coat before Good Queen Bess, and has been immortalized for his chivalry, but I think a more courtly deed was that of the gallant Irishman Pat Cleburne. For one was kowtowing before royalty and the other had in his heart only thoughtfulness and humanity for the common man afoot."

Concluding his dramatic and emotional speech he told his highly responsive audience of North American Irish: "The lost Irish tribes of the South are not lost; they are not lost any more than the 'wild geese' that flew across the Channel from Ireland were lost. They are not lost any more than the McMahons who went to France, or the O'Connells who went to Spain, or the Simon Bolivars who went to South America, or the O'Farrels and the O'Briens who went to Cuba. For their Irish blood is of the strain that cannot be extinguished and it lives today, thank God, in the attributes and the habits and the customs and the traditions of the Southern people."

The Irish and Canada

It is not generally known that Irish fishermen were putting down their nets off Newfoundland as early as 1595! Many Irish fishermen settled in Newfoundland in the 1700s, and one third of the population of Nova Scotia is of Irish descent. The Irish fishermen came mainly from Waterford, Tipperary and Wexford. The failure of the 1798 Rising, and the subsequent excesses of the Yeomanry in Ireland, sent thousands to Canada, and the famine of 1822 brought more settlers in ever increasing numbers. Today there are over one and a half million Canadians who can reckon to be of Irish descent.

To escape the famines in Ireland great numbers came in 1846. Over 32,000 landed in Montreal in Quebec, and the following year over 70,000 came. The tragedy was that the majority of them, already suffering from the effects of starvation, came from the crowded hulks of the "coffin" ships, bearing with them the last stages of cholera, and burial in mass graves on the shore became the fate of many. Some ten thousand Irish bodies have made a corner of a Canadian field far greener than any green field abandoned in Ireland .... The famines, and the subsequent emigration schemes of the British Government, were a gift to the landlord class in Ireland, enabling them to get rid of "disaffected" tenants. The lords of Cork were to the fore in this terrible trafficking in humanity, and cheerfully cleared whole townlands and villages. The lords, whose infamous names are written large on the pages of Irish history, included Lord Kingston of the barony of Fermoy in County Cork – you can still see the walls of his one-time estate near Mitchelstown – who forcibly removed thousands of individuals from Fermoy, Ballyhooly, Mallow, Kildorrey, Charleville and Kilworth. As magistrates, the landlords did not hesitate to transport five hundred at a time to Quebec.

The chief architects in this inhuman traffic were, in addition to Lord Kingston, Lord Mount Cashell of Kilworth, Lord Doneraile and Lord Ennismore. Kingston shifted 1,600 people in one go, and each lord was responsible for up to two thousand individuals being transported from their estates. Already suffering from smallpox and typhus and from near starvation, most died after the revolting sea journey. Some became log cabin settlers in the newfound wilderness, although, coming from the boglands of Ireland, they had never held an axe in their hands, and knew nothing about clearing forest for habitation. Some became navvies and worked on the canals or the railroads. Most came from the desolate, hungry wilds of Munster and Connacht, and worked in gangs of county groups.

Canada was often a "back door" for those Irish emigrants who survived to move on to the United States. Because so many of these poor people were very sick, Grosse Isle, on the St. Lawrence River at the entrance to the city of Quebec, became a quarantine island in 1834. Many a valiant priest and doctor fell mortally ill after tending to the needs of the dying famine victims.

It is a deeply moving experience to stand before a large, simple, unhewn stone, erected in 1859 by Irish railroad navvies constructing the railway bridge in Montreal, where they discovered the bones of their fellow countrymen, women and children, who were buried in mass graves on the site of the old emigration sheds at Point St. Charles. The inscription on the rough boulder reads:

"Preserve from Desecration
The remains of 600 emigrants
who died of ships fever AD 1847-8
This stone is erected by the workmen of
Messrs Peto, Brassey and Betts
Employed in the construction of the
Victoria Bridge AD 1859"

Another simple and moving epitaph can be found on Grosse Isle where, in 1909, the Ancient Order of Hibernians erected a Celtic cross:

"Sacred to the memory of thousands of Irish immigrants who, to preserve the faith, suffered hunger and exile in 1847-48 and stricken with fever ended here there sorrowful pilgrimage."

And yet many Irish Canadians survived, and every year, on March 17th, the Irish Society of Montreal has one of the most spectacular St. Patrick's Day parades in the world, with the reviewing stand packed with civic dignitaries, including the Irish ambassador, and with Royal Canadian Air Force jets flying over the parade in salute.

Those who survived made good in many places. From 1823 to 1825 emigrants, mostly from Munster, made their homes in Upper Canada in settlements such as Peterborough, Lanark, Renfrew, Carleton and Northumberland. In 1826 some 20,000 settled in the Lake Erie district alone. The Orangemen from Ulster headed mainly for Toronto.

That a native-born Irishman could go right to the top of Canadian politics can best be seen in the career of Thomas D'Arcy McGhee, Irish poet and statesman. He was born in the "wee" county, County Louth, in Carlingford, on April 13th, 1825, and educated by "hedge" schoolmasters in County Wexford. His mother's family had strong connections with the insurrection of 1798, and she instilled in him a deep love of Ireland. In 1842 he emigrated to Quebec, and drifted down to Boston, where he became a journalist on *The Boston Pilot*. In 1845, he returned to his native land and worked on *The Freeman's Journal*, and also wrote for *The Nation*. He was active in the Young Ireland movement, was arrested, and fled to Philaclelphia in 1848, and resumed journalism in Boston, where he soon fell foul of the Catholic clergy because of his political beliefs.

In 1857 McGhee moved to Montreal, invited there by the Irish Society to edit the publication *The New Era*. Due to the political influence of Daniel O'Connell, he became less of a rebel and more of a constitutionalist, and his political thinking for Canada was far in advance of his time. He developed the idea for a new Canadian nationality, and suggested a federal system of government. He argued for the development of Canadian culture and literature, as opposed to the swamping of Canada by American culture and literature. He was elected to represent Montreal in the Legislative Assembly, backed by the St. Patrick's Society of Montreal, and he went on to become Minister for Agriculture, Immigration and Statistics in 1863. He sought and promoted social, political and religious freedom for Irish Canadians. He was opposed to the Fenian doctrine of physical force and denounced the Fenian invasion of Canada, which had been based on the assumption that Irish Canadians would rally to their cause. This, however, was his undoing and sealed his fate, for on April 7th, 1868, when he was almost forty-three years of age, he was assassinated by a fellow Irishman, James Whelan, a Fenian who shot him, was tried, found guilty of murder, and publicly hanged in Ottawa on February 11th, 1869.

Canada has always opened its vast doors to those desirous of starting a new way of life. For example, it provided a haven of refuge for Captain J.C. Bowen-Colthurst, who had the pacifist Francis Sheehy Skeffington arrested while he was trying to stop looting during the 1916 rising in Dublin. Sheehy Skeffington, after a drumhead court-martial, was executed on the orders of his fellow Irishman, Bowen-Colthurst, ending the life of the thirty-eight-year old supporter of the suffragette movement, who, as a close friend of James Joyce, had featured as a character in *A Portrait of the Artist as a Young Man*.

The Irish and Australia

Sometimes, in wandering among the tombstones of an old English country churchyard on the south coast overlooking the English Channel, one comes across the headstone of a Royal Naval veteran who sailed the South Seas with Captain Cook, who discovered Australia. It is worth remembering that the voyages of Captain Cook were contemporary with the War of American Independence – King George, and his equally incompetent ministers, such as Lord George Germain, the Secretary of War, contributed greatly to the loss of the American Colonies, which had become a dumping ground over the years for British convicts until 1776.

Cook discovered New South Wales in 1770, finding a continent occupied by a small native population of aborigines, which even today numbers only 200,000. It was conveniently ripe for white settlement, and, in 1783, the British Secretary of State decided to switch the transportation of convicts from America to New South Wales. The first convict expedition, 750 in number, set sail for Australia in 1787, under the command of Captain Phillip of the Royal Navy, who was to act as the first Governor. In January, 1788, the marines guarding the prisoners became the first free settlers in Botany Bay. This site was then abandoned in favor of Port Jackson, and in honor of Lord Sydney, the British Home Secretary, the new settlement of Sydney was named, and set up as a military state.

By 1790 Europe was in the turmoil of the French Revolution, and in 1798 Ireland had risen in one of its periodic revolts, which was viciously put down by the redcoats, assisted by Hessian mercenaries. Broadly speaking, the Ireland of those days could be seen as an English garrison, run from Dublin Castle. The peasantry of Ireland was at the mercy of a largely debauched, drunken and dissolute landlord class which had the power to be judge, jury and executioner – or transporter – of any of its tenants, be they political thinkers or anyone who stepped out of line in any way. The all-powerful magistrate class sentenced hundreds of people – men and women – without trial to transportation in convict ships to Botany Bay. They were often sentenced for life, their "crimes" unnamed, and seldom, if ever, written down.

The first English prisoners had landed in 1788, and in 1791, Irish prisoners started to arrive, thus forging the first Irish-Australian links. Ireland was then a nation up in arms and in desperate political turmoil, and the first prison ships contained many simple country folk, driven in desperation to political "crimes." For many it became, under military goading, a choice of transportation for life, or hanging by the neck or even suicide. The convict ships themselves were not much better than the old Negro slave ships, as frequently the convicts were kept in irons throughout a horrendous six-month voyage, during which they suffered hunger, thirst, the lash and harassment from their captains and crews. In those days flogging was a normal form of discipline in both the British Navy and the British Army, and brutality was the only way in which the officers could effectively govern and control the lower-deck and lesser orders.

It was not until as late as 1886 that the flogging of soldiers was abolished in the British Army, and then only because of a case in which a man was flogged to death, and the British Army doctors tried to cover it up by saying that the soldier had died of pneumonia!

Not all the Irish convicts were poor folk or agricultural laborers, for, after the rebellion of 1798, Presbyterian ministers and professional men, such as doctors, were among the more educated revolutionaries to be transported. Many of the early political prisoners were Presbyterian ministers from County Derry, County Down and County Antrim. Very soon, Irish convicts formed a large percentage of the prisoner population in Australia, and the authorities were greatly concerned at their numbers, their escape attempts, their standard of intelligence, and the fact that Catholic priests as well as Presbyterian ministers were among the arrivals. For the military authorities' answer to most problems was violence – either shooting recalcitrant prisoners, flogging them into submission, or allowing them to die of overwork and under-nourishment. The bewildered convicts, separated from their home and country, their wives and families, and ignorant of their ultimate fate, all too often tried to escape. The authorities, desperate to control the colony, regularly executed "trouble makers" by hanging them publicly, and any escaped convicts who were unlucky enough to be recaptured were certain to face a flogging before the hangman's noose. Flogging could mean two or three hundred lashes, which left a man's back cut open to the bone, and the flesh of his buttocks and legs reduced to pulp, everything short of actually being flogged to death being permitted .... Frequently a doctor was present to see just how far the torture could be allowed to go.

The beautiful harbor of Cork was the normal point of departure for convict ships from Ireland to Australia, and the public records of correspondence between Dublin Castle and the Governor in Australia give details of regular shiploads of convicts. The rebels of 1798 were followed by the rebels of 1803, and one of the more famous characters to be transported to Botany Bay was the United Irishman, Michael Dwyer of County Wicklow. He had been on the run in the Wicklow mountains, with his partisan comrades Hugh Byrne, Samuel McAllister and Martin Bourke. He was ready to join in the 1803 Dublin rising, led by Robert Emmet, and finally surrendered to the authorities in Dublin Castle. In return for giving themselves up voluntarily, Michael Dwyer, Hugh Byrne, Martin Bourke and Arthur Devlin expected to be permitted to go into exile to America. To their horror they found themselves transported to Botany Bay, and to the tender mercies of the Governor, the notorious Captain Bligh of "Bounty" fame – a cruel, vicious devil of a man.

In 1807, the infamous Captain Bligh (who, incidentally, lies buried in Lambeth Palace graveyard in London, beside the River Thames) arrested Michael Dwyer and his comrades on trumped up charges of insurrection. Dwyer was sent to Van Diemen's Land (now Tasmania) for six months, and his comrades were sent to other settlements, to split them up. The bloodthirsty Bligh was eventually deposed as Governor and Dwyer was allowed to return to Sydney, where he was appointed Constable, and given a grant of land – as were his comrades – by the more civilized and humane Governor who had replaced Bligh. Dwyer died in the 1820s, but his wife Mary lived on in Sydney to the ripe old age of ninety five.

Throughout the nineteenth century, convict ships regularly set sail from Cork to Sydney. Many of those transported were Catholics who found, on arrival in their penal settlements, that the Church of Rome was not recognized, and they were obliged to attend state religious services of the Protestant faith. Although there were priests among the early convicts, they were not allowed to perform their religious duties and it was not until 1803 that the first Catholic priest was permitted to celebrate mass on Sundays for Catholic convicts, in a peculiar offical climate where "no Popery" was the order of the day. Appropriately enough, on the site of the house in Sydney where the first Catholic service was held, there now stands the Catholic Church of Saint Patrick.

The rebellions of 1798 and 1803 in Ireland, land of insurrection, were followed by the rising of the Young Ireland movement in 1848. By this time the disastrous famine years of 1845 to 1848 had halved the population of Ireland by starvation and emigration. The leaders of the Young Ireland movement were an entirely new type of revolutionary, coming from the middle class, the merchants and the professions, and driven to rebellion by the callousness of the absentee landlord class – the squires and the gobeen men – who feasted on the results of the famine, as their lands were more profitable when populated by sheep and cattle rather than people. The most remarkable leader of the 1848 rising was John Mitchel, born in 1815 in Dungiven, County Derry. The son of a Presbyterian minister, and a law graduate of the College of the Holy and Undivided Trinity in Dublin, he became editor of *The Nation*, the journal of the Young Ireland movement, and eventually founded his own newspaper, *The United Irishman*. He was greatly influenced by the political writings of James Fintian Lalor, who advocated resistance by the starving tenants against their avaricious landlords, their agents, and the establishment in Dublin Castle which protected these interests. Because of his revolutionary writings, Mitchel was arrested in Dublin and, under a hastily arranged Treason Felony Act, he was sentenced to fourteen years transportation to Van Diemen's Land (Tasmania).

He wrote an account of his days as a political prisoner in Australia in his now famous *Jail Journal or Five Years in British Prisons*. He escaped to America in 1853, and his journal was first published as a series of newspaper articles in New York a year later.

The opening pages of *Jail Journal* recount how he bade farewell to his wife and two small boys before being carried off in chains. He was taken from Dublin by ship to Spike Island, the prison in Cork harbor, and from there, via Bermuda and the Cape of Good Hope, to Van Diemen's Land. In the sixth chapter of his remarkable work he describes the scourging with the cat o'nine tails of three convicts who were recaptured after an escape bid from the ship. He writes movingly of the suffering of the two hundred or so Irish prisoners on the ship, many of them boys aged between twelve and seventeen: "… traversing the deep under bayonet-points, to be shot out like rubbish on a bare foreign strand amongst a people whose very language they knew not." The latter reference is to the fact that many were native Irish speakers, with no knowledge of English.

It took five months to reach the Cape, and it was not until April, 1850, that Mitchel first saw the mountainous southern coast of Van Diemen's Land, where he was a "ticket-of-leave" man in the village of Bothwell, forty-six miles from Hobart. To his utter amazement he found a fellow prisoner, Patrick O'Donoughue, editing a newspaper in Hobart called the *The Irish Exile.* In Bothwell he was allowed to team up with another United Irishman – John Martin, a journalist school friend who was born in 1812, in Loughorne, County Down. He too had been transported for "Treason-Felony" and was exiled to Tasmania from 1849 to 1854. He later returned to Ireland where he became the Member of Parliament for County Meath in 1871. Charles Stewart Parnell succeeded him.

Mitchel gives a fascinating description of his days in exile, where his fellow conspirators were segregated in police areas. The English and Scottish settlers were fair-minded men who refused to regard him or his associates as felons. The convict class were taboo among the free settlers, but political prisoners were accepted into normal society, and rode horses, hunted kangaroo and farmed. They also met fellow rebels, such as Terence Bellew MacManus from County Fermanagh, who was a prosperous shipping agent in Liverpool, and who was sentenced to death for his part in the Ballingarry insurrection attempt in County Tipperary. His death sentence was commuted to transportation to Van Diemen's Land, from whence he escaped to America, in 1852, with Francis Meagher –"Meagher of the Sword."

This Young Irelander was born in County Waterford, in a house which is now the well-known Granville Hotel and which today boasts a "Thomas Francis Meagher Room." Meagher became a lawyer and a journalist. He was dubbed "Meagher of the Sword" by William Makepeace Thackery because of a historic fighting speech he made in Dublin defending recourse to the sword in the liberation of Ireland. He was educated by the Jesuits in Clongowes Wood College, near the village of Clane in the County of Kildare and then, as his wealthy merchant father from Waterford regarded Trinity College as anti-Irish and anti-Catholic, at the Jesuit College of Stonyhurst in England, where he studied philosophy. His background and education abroad, both in England and in France, made him particularly broad-minded, despite a fierce and ardent nationalism. In writing of his voyage as a prisoner on HMS *Swift* bound for Australia, he speaks of the officers and men as "frank, generous, warm-hearted, and of gallant bravery," a sharp contrast to the "cold, cramped rigidity" of some of the officials in the penal colony. His impressions of Australia, however, are full of admiration: "In most, if not all, those features which constitute the

strength, the wealth, and grandeur of a country, it has been endowed. The seas which encompass it, the lakes and rivers which refresh and fertilise, the woods which shadow, and the genial sky which arches it – all bear testimony to the excellence of the Divine Hand, and with sounds of the finest harmony, with signs of the brightest colouring, proclaim the goodness and munificence of heaven on its behalf. The climate is more than healthful. It is invigorating and inspiring … Oh! to think that a land so blest – so rich in all that makes life pleasant, beautiful and great – so formed to be a refuge and a sweet abiding place, in these latter times, for the younger children of the old, decrepit, worn-out world at home – to think that such a land is doomed to be the prison, the workhouse and the grave, of the Empire's outcast poverty, ignorance and guilt!"

In America, Meagher had the distinction of being the man to form New York's famous Irish Brigade – the Fighting 69th – which fought nobly under its green-and-gold harp flag at Bull Run, Fort Sumter, Fredericksburgh and Chancellorsville. Annihilated at Gettysburg in 1863, the regiment was re-formed to fight again. Meagher held the rank of Lieutenant General, and became Acting Governor of Montana. Today his uniform, sword and flag are on display in Ireland, in the Council Chamber of the Waterford City Hall, and he is remembered by his statue in Helena, the capital city of the State of Montana.

While Meagher was Governor of Montana, his honesty in public life made him many enemies, particularly among professional politicians on the make at the expense of the public. His death was a mystery, as it occured while he was on official business at Fort Benton when he went aboard a steamer, moored in the river, to rest for the night. During the night his cry was heard, and he was presumed to have accidentally fallen overboard, and to have drowned. An assassin did confess to having murdered him, but then withdrew his confession and, like the death of President John F. Kennedy more recently, the real cause of his death has never been fully explained.

Another famous Young Irelander to join John Mitchel and his companions in the land of the kangaroo and duck-billed platypus was Kevin Izod O'Doherty who was born in Dublin in 1823. He was transported for his part in the rising of 1848, and became a doctor, working in the hospital of St. Mary s in Hobart. He organized the escape to America of his friend John Mitchel, and on his release from the convict settlement in 1855, he studied at the Royal College of Surgeons in Dublin, and was made a Fellow in 1857. He married Eva Kelly, "Eva" the poetess of *The Nation* and returned to Australia. He was elected a member of the Legislative Assembly of Queensland while a doctor in Brisbane, but eventually died in poverty in 1905, a sad fate for a gifted man.

Among the extraordinary leaders of the abortive Young Ireland uprising in 1848 was William Smith O'Brien, who was born in 1803 in the County of Clare, in Dromoland Castle, the ancestral home of the O'Brien clan of Clare. Educated at Harrow and at Trinity College,

Cambridge, he became Member of Parliament for Ennis, County Clare, from 1828 to 1841. After backing the parliamentarian Daniel O'Connell, he was so moved by the plight of the starving peasantry that he supported the rising in Ballingarry in County Tipperary. He was arrested, and condemned to death, but his sentence was commuted to transportation to Van Diemens Land. After eight years as a convict in Australia, he was released and returned to Ireland. He retired from public affairs and died in Bangor, Wales, in 1864, one of the last survivors of what the history books have come to call the "Battle of Widow McCormack's cabbage patch," in Ballingarry.

John Mitchel, the king-pin of the convicts in exile in Australia, was joined by his wife and family in Van Diemen's Land, and describes in *Jail Journal* the first election of representatives under the new Constitution – one-third Crown nominees and two-thirds elected by the people. This was the beginning of the end for corrupt governors and their gangs of highly-paid officials. During these elections, John Mitchel met, quite by accident, William Smith O'Brien, and his description is something the history books do not usually portray: "He seems evidently sinking in health; his form is hardly so erect, nor his step so stately; his hair is more grizzled, and his face bears traces of pain and passion. It is sad to look upon this noblest of Irishmen, thrust in here among the off-scourings of England's gaols, with his home desolated, and his hopes ruined, and his defeated life falling into the sere and yellow leaf. He is fifty years of age, yet has all the high and intense pleasure of youth in these majestic hills and woods, softened, indeed, and made pensive by sorrow and haunted by the ghosts of buried hopes. He is a rare and noble sight to see; a man who cannot be crushed, bowed, or broken ...." Such is the portrait of an Irish revolutionary in the setting of Australia.

In his *Journal* on October 14th, 1850, Mitchel gives this description of a non-convict Irish settler family: "This morning we took a conveyance, a sort of spring cart, and drove sixteen miles through the valley of the Macquairie river, the Sugar-loaf, where dwells a worthy Irish family, emigrants of thirty two years ago from the County of Cork. Their name is Connell. We had promised to visit them on our way back from Avoca; and Mr Connell had kindly sent for our horses to Oatlands, and has them ready for our ride tomorrow up to the lakes. Mr Connell and his wife have had severe hardships in their early days of settlement – a wild forest to tame and convert into green fields – wilder black natives to watch and keep guard against – and wildest convict bushrangers to fight, sometimes in their own house. Mrs Connell is a thorough Celtic Irish woman – has the Munster accent as fresh as if she had left Cork last year, and is, in short, as genuine an Irish Vanithee or 'Woman of the House' as you will find in Ireland at this day – perhaps more so – for Carthagenian 'civilization' has been closer and more deadly in its embrace among the valleys of Munster, than it could be among the wilds of the Sugar-loaf forests. Most of their laborious toil and struggle is over: their farm smiles with green corn fields, and their sheep whiten their pastures; their banks are well furnished with bees, and Mrs Connell's mead is seductive; the black Tasmanians have all disappeared before convict civilization; and even the bushrangers are not 'out' so often these late years. Still it is needful that every lonely house should be well supplied with arms."

Mitchel also describes the "rural population" in pursuit of the kangaroo and opossum to procure a few shillings for their skins to invest in rum and a little gambling. "Rural population! It is almost profane to apply the title to these rascals. All the shepherds and stock-keepers, without exception, are convicts – many of them thrice convicted convicts! There is no peasantry. Very few of them have wives, still fewer families, and the fewer the better. Their wives are clearly transported women, too: shop-lifters, prostitutes, pickpockets, and other such sweepings of the London pavements. Yet, after all, what a strange animal is man! The best shepherds in Van Diemen's Land are London thieves – men who never saw a live sheep before they were transported, and what is stranger still, many of them grow rather decent – it would be too strong to say honest – by the mere contact with mother earth here. They are friendly to one another and hospitable to strangers."

Mitchel was helped in the final stages of his escape by the English son of a local magistrate, and accepted on the run by Tasmanians of English ancestry who had "a sincere regard for Irish rebels." In Port Sorel, Bass's Straits, he was given sanctuary by Irish farmer emigrants who had been evicted by Lord Hawarden from his estates in County Tipperary. Disguised as a priest, Mitchel made his way to Sydney, then a beautiful seaport town of 80,000 inhabitants, and thence, via Tahiti, to San Francisco, and on to New York where he worked as a journalist, and then to Tennessee, where he farmed.

He finally returned to Ireland in 1874, and was elected MP for Tipperary, but was not allowed to take his seat in the House of Commons because he was a convicted felon and an escaped convict. He died in Newry in 1875.

Tasmania, as Van Diemen's Land is called today, is now Australia's sixth and smallest state, slightly smaller than Ireland, which ceased receiving convict transports in 1853. It is an island of great natural beauty, of lush pastures and rich pastoral land, which was the salvation of many an early settler evicted from his cabbage patch in Ireland in the bad old days of the landlords of Victorian times.

Not all the leaders of the Young Ireland Rising of 1848 were sentenced to death, and that sentence commuted to transportation to Van Diemen's Land. Sir Charles Gavan Duffy was the exception. Born in County Monaghan in 1816, and educated at Monaghan Public School and the Royal Belfast Academical Institute, he founded the newspaper *The Belfast Vindicator* and then moved to Dublin to found *The Nation* with Thomas

Davis and John Blake Dillon. The object of the journalists on *The Nation* was to get the people off their knees, and to strike back against the landlord class that had a life-and-death hold over them. The writings of Gavan Duffy that roused the people against Dublin Castle, and his active part in the Ballingarry Rising of 1848, put him on trial for sedition. He was arrested and tried five times, and his paper suppressed. Despite packed juries, rewarded well financially by Dublin Castle, or even with jobs as "Castle Hacks," the jury in the final trial disagreed. One lone noble character of a juror, Mr Martin Burke, founder and proprietor of the Shelbourne Hotel in St. Stephen's Green, Dublin, steadfastly held out in favor of the prisoner, and the case for the prosecution had to be dropped. It was a courageous thing to do for a newly emerging hotelier who relied on Dublin's wealthy ruling class for much of his livelihood. His bravery deserves a plaque to his memory in the hotel which still stands today.

Gavan Duffy went on to become Member of Parliament for New Ross, County Wexford, and tiring of the near farce of parliamentary democracy, he emigrated to Australia in 1856. He became active in public life there, was made Prime Minister of Victoria, and was knighted in 1873. While Martin Burke may not have a commemorative plaque in the Shelbourne Hotel today, he lives on in the pages of a book by Gavan Duffy, published in 1898; *My Life in Two Hemispheres*. Proprietor of an hotel frequented by the gentry, Mr Burke proved not only a steadfast juror but a constitutional student of uncommon force. Lord Brougham attacked him savagely in the House of Lords, and he replied in a letter vindicating the rights of a juror, with notable knowledge, vigor and courtesy.

Sir Gavan Duffy died in Nice in 1903. His son, George, became a noted lawyer and Nationalist politician in more recent Irish history.

For the Young Ireland leaders, being sentenced to transportation as convict felons to an unknown land some ten thousand miles from home and family, was an enormous price to pay for opposing the debauched and degraded political system run from Dublin Castle. To better understand the motives of the young Irelanders, John Mitchel quotes from Meagher's speech to his judges at Clonmel: "The history of Ireland explains my crime and justifies it. No man proudly mounts the scaffold, or coolly faces a felon's death, or walks with his head high and defiance on his tongue into the cell of a convict hulk for nothing. No man, let him be as 'young' and as 'vain' as you will, can do this in the wantoness of youth or the intoxication of vanity."

As always, Irish political prisoners were at their most eloquent when faced with the high jump!

Mitchel, throughout his *Journal*, gives snapshot accounts of the local inhabitants. For example, while out riding one day in the police district to which he was confined, he came across a convict barrack "… and as we follow the winding of the road through that mountain glen, we meet parties of miserable wretches harnessed to gravel carts, and drawing the same under the orders of an overseer. The men are dressed in piebald suits of yellow and grey, and with their hair close cropped, their close leathern caps, and hang-dog countenances were a most evil, rueful and abominable aspect."

He manages to capture the dejection and horror of another scene: "We overtake on our track homeward, a man and a woman – the woman, a hideous and obscene-looking creature, with a brandy blotched face, and a white satin bonnet, adorned with artificial flowers. She is a pass-holding servant, just discharged from some remote settlers house, and she is going to Hobart Town, in custody. The man is a convict constable: he carries a musket on his shoulders, and his blue frock coat is girt by a belt, on which hang and jingle a pair of handcuffs."

The Australia of the 1850s had a remarkably free and independent Press, which regularly wrote in favor of the "Irish State Prisoners," and took the authorities to task for their petty persecutions of their captives. Under a false sentence, after a "trial" by a packed jury, the Irish political prisoners were neither true convicts nor treated like the thousands of ticket-of-leave holders who could live where they pleased, and only had to report twice a year to the police. Irish political prisoners were obliged to give a parole not to try to escape from their police area. Their correspondence was subjected to censorship and they lived a kind of "open-prison" life, never quite knowing their future.

After three years in exile in Van Diemen's Land, Mitchel writes in a light-hearted and witty manner of his life on the farm:

"January 5th, 1853, – I am prosecuting my hay harvest diligently, with the aid of two or three horrible convict cut-throats, all from Ireland – and all, by their own account, transported for seizing arms. This is considered among these fellows a respectable sort of offence. The rascals can earn ten British shillings per diem at harvest-time and they live all the year round like Irish kings, not to speak of Irish cut-throats. They don't like to work too hard, and require a good deal of time. They come early from their work, smoke and chat with one another all evening in the yard, and go to sleep in their opossum rugs in the barn. Yet, with all this high reward they receive for their crimes, this paternal care to make thieving happy, and munificent endowment of rascality, the creatures are not utterly bad – not half as bad for example, as the Queen of England's Cabinet counsellors. They are civil, good natured with one another and not thievish at all – partly because they are so well off that there is little temptation, and partly because the punishments are savage."

As Mitchel finally headed for freedom he wrote of his island prison: "Adieu then, beauteous island, full of sorrow and gnashing of teeth – Island of fragrant forests and bright rivers and fair women! – Island of chains and scourges, and blind, brutal rage and passion! Behind those far blue peaks, in many a green valley known to me, dwell some of the best and warm-hearted of all God's creatures." A fair enough tribute to some of the first families to settle in Australia.

Not all the early Irish settlers in Australia were there

for political reasons and one of the most famous exceptions was the explorer Robert O'Hara Burke. He was born in St. Cleran, in County Galway, in 1820, the son of a British Army officer. He was educated in Belgium, joined the Austrian Army, and attained the rank of Captain. He later returned to Ireland and joined the Royal Irish Constabulary. Restless, like many an Irishman, he emigrated to Australia, and became an Inspector of Police in the state of Victoria. When the state decided to explore the continent he was chosen to lead one of the first expeditions because of his military and commanding background.

Many intrepid explorers worked at opening up the interior of the great continent, and all suffered from the immense drought and tropical heat. The Robert O'Hara Burke expedition was no exception. Financed by the state and by popular appeal, the expedition purchased camels, horses and supplies, and picked the men who were to attempt the crossing of the unknown continent from Victoria in the south to the Gulf of Carpentaria in the north, some fifteen degrees south of the equator. Leaving Melbourne, Burke and his team of experts set out to be the first white men to cross the vast continent from south to north. The expedition left in August 1860, and a month later reached Menindee on the River Darling. Already the camel expert had left the party, in high dudgeon at the attitude of the impetuous Irish leader of the expedition, who had rashly decided to push on into the unknown, uncharted outback. Not waiting for the main support of his expedition, Burke and two companions with their horses and camels and several months' supplies, headed north for Eyre Creek in Queensland. Crossing the Tropic of Capricorn they reached the Cloncurry and the Flinders rivers, and they viewed the northern seas before starting on their return journey. Four months into the new year they missed the back up party at Cooper's Creek. Again the impatient Burke decided to press on and complete the remainder of the return journey by a different route. By May their last camel was dead and they were near starvation in the wilderness. By the end of June the deputy leader of the expedition was dead; Burke died later of starvation, and only John King survived.

Although this remarkable journey was technically a failure, the citizens of Melbourne were deeply moved by the gallantry of the captain from Galway, and erected a monument to his heroic memory. The monument features statues of Burke and his companion, William Wills. His ill-fated and badly managed foray into the unknown inspired many to follow his exploratory zeal and open up the interior of Australia.

In the time of Robert O'Hara Burke and his companions, such pioneer expeditions of exploration knew little or nothing of the existence or whereabouts or customs of the native aboriginal inhabitants of the outback. Burke's party, on their outward journey, was given sustenance by them on one occasion, when they were lost and without food. The expedition's sole survivor, Irishman John King, owed his life to the natives who took care of him for several months, feeding him on native plants unknown to white men.

Today, the once uncharted and unknown outback is a tourist attraction with air-conditioned coaches traveling to see the rock cuttings and drawings of the Australian aboriginals, who carefully preserve their sacred rocks and caves and mysterious folklore – their places as holy to them as any Christian holy shrine is to us. Nevertheless, all too little is known of the folklore and worship of the original native inhabitants.

For the first Irish settlers in Australia, it must have been an extraordinary change to see kangaroo, wallabies, emus, the black swan, the duck-billed platypus and a thousand different species of fish – a sharp contrast to the Emerald Isle.

Comparatively unknown in our history books is the Irish leader and political thinker, James Fintan Lalor, whose writings, teachings and actions played a considerable part in the land war in Ireland of the 1840s, and whose gospel of the land for the people had a profound influence on Australian politics in the 1850s. Lalor, born in 1807 in Tenakill, in Queen's County (now County Laois), suffered all his life from a congenital spine disease. He evolved a political outlook which caused him to teach that "the ownership of Ireland, moral and material is vested right in the people of Ireland."

This doctrine of the land for the people was revolutionary, and Lalor began agitating for the withholding of rents from their landlords by the famine stricken people. He himself was a working farmer – when not in prison for his views. Lalor's political views were nurtured and cherished until the time of James Connolly, the leader of the 1916 Rising. His immediate circle of friends included the militants of the Young Irelanders, such as John Mitchel, John Martin, Charles Gavan Duffy, and the revolutionaries Thomas Clark Luby, John O'Leary and Charles J. Kickham. His father, Patrick, was his inspiration, as he had led his fellow farmers in the 1830s to fight the Tithe War against the system whereby the Church of England clergymen in Ireland gleaned from the wretched tenantry a crippling contribution to their excellent standard of living. Both Presbyterian and Catholic tillage farmers were inflicted with this unjust burden, collected by the Protestant parsons' agents with the utmost severity. The ragged, destitute tenants occasionally fought with scythes and pitchforks against the might of the establishment, and the established church, which did not represent their religion, and which could call out the military to collect the tithes. Patrick Lalor, as Member of Parliament for Queen's County, fought a magnificent battle against the tithe system in the House of Commons. James Lalor, like a Ghandi of his time, called for civil disobedience and passive resistance on a massive scale. And the government of Westminster actually listened to the pleadings of MP Patrick Lalor, and eventually lifted the crushing burden of the tithe system. James went further and took up a revolutionary stance which called for the total freedom of Ireland from British rule.

One of his younger brothers, Peter, born in 1823 in

Tenakill, studied at Trinity College, Dublin, and like many of his fellow Irishmen, emigrated quite freely to Australia in 1852, with one of his many brothers. They became successful merchants in Melbourne, and when the great gold finds were made in Ballarat, Peter, together with many young men from Ireland, headed off to seek his fortune. It did not turn out quite the way he had intended. Gold had been found in 1851 at Bathurst in New South Wales, and now, in 1858, at Ballarat and Bendigo in Victoria. Thousands of immigrants, many of them Irish, poured into Australia, and the population of Victoria increased fivefold in five years. The world's imagination was fired by gold fever, and while the transportation of convicts had ceased by 1853, Australia was the object of all sorts of emigration schemes, bringing to its shores a young, turbulent, freedom-seeking people, who were to become the foundation of democracy in the great continent.

Ballarat, from being a small village of a few hundred people, suddenly became a town of tens of thousands of gold miners. The miners paid the government a prospector's licence fee, and although they were allowed to prospect for the world's most precious metal, they had no voting rights in their land of opportunity, and felt this needed changing. The miners sought what might today be termed civil rights, and organized themselves into a political Reform League. On November 30th, 1854, on Bakery Hill at Ballarat, thousands of miners assembled in a protest against the government licence fee. The scene was set for an inevitable confrontation between the military forces of the government, and the muscle of the men, who were without articulate leadership. On the previous day, some ten thousand miners had assembled under the diggers' flag of the Southern Cross, a blue flag with white stars. On November 30th one clash with the military resulted in a "digger" being killed and some prisoners being taken.

Peter Lalor, in the tradition of his father and his brother, was stirred by the gathering: "I looked around me, I saw brave and honest men who had come thousands of miles to labour for independence. I knew that hundreds were in great poverty who would possess health and happiness if allowed to cultivate the wilderness which surrounded us. The grievances under which we had long suffered, and the brutal attack of that day, flashed across my mind; and with the burning feelings of an injured man I mounted the stand and proclaimed liberty."

He offered to assume the leadership of the diggers saying that, while he had no pretentions of military knowledge, he would lead the defense of the miners in their fight for their rights and liberties. Lalor addressed the diggers and called for a plan to defend themselves from the police and the military on the gravel pits. The men built a wooden stockade around the Eureka mine shaft, and stocked up with arms and ammunition, mainly sporting guns, revolvers, pitchforks and pikes. The Defense Council was led by a Clare man, John Diamond. A Father Patrick Smythe, from County Mayo,

led a parly with the Commissioner of Police and the local magistrate, and called upon the diggers to avoid bloodshed. But the diggers, some 1,500 of them, stood their ground under the flag of the Southern Cross, and their password was "Vinegar Hill," after the famous insurgent battle in Wexford in 1798. The cavalry and military from Melbourne stormed the Eureka Stockade on the Sunday morning, and overwhelmed the mainly Irish rebels, killing fourteen, and wounding a dozen or more. Peter Lalor had his left arm shot off, and was given sanctuary by Father Smythe, and then hidden in the home of his fiancée Alicia Dunn. Thirteen diggers were arrested and put on trial, most of them Irish, but no jury would convict them. The miners raised a special fund for Peter Lalor, with which he purchased 160 acres of good land, ten miles from Ballarat. The dead were mourned in County Clare, in Kilkenny and in Donegal, and the wounded came from six different counties in Ireland.

In 1855, Lalor was elected as a representative of Ballarat in the Parliament of Victoria, and became Postmaster-General and Speaker of the House. He died in February, 1889, and lies buried in Melbourne General Cemetery. A noble obelisk now stands in memory of the Eureka Stockade Uprising, a memorial which names both diggers and soldiers who fell in the making of a chapter of Australian history, "an affirmation of Australian nationhood and Australian Democracy."

Fremantle in Western Australia, over eleven thousand miles from home, was to be the last port in Australia to receive Irish political prisoners in January 1868, sixty-three of them, after the ill-fated Fenian Rising of 1867. The Fenians were an Irish Republican brotherhood, a secret society dedicated to fight for the freedom of Ireland using physical force. One of the most resilient of their leaders was John Boyle O'Reilly, born in Dowth Castle in County Louth in 1848, who was sentenced to death for his political activities, a sentence which was commuted to twenty years in jail. After enormous hardship and suffering in the Millbank prison in London, in Portsmouth prison and in Dartmoor, to his great surprise, he and sixty-two other political prisoners found themselves on the last convict ship bound for Australia, *The Hougoumont*. He and his gang worked as road builders in Bunbury, and just one year later he made his escape to Boston, where he became editor and owner of that excellent paper, *The Boston Pilot*. His comrades went in different directions. Under an amnesty, half of them were eventually released, and most returned home to Ireland, or sought sanctuary in America. A handful stayed in Australia, and became contractors, teachers, businessmen and journalists. They set up homes in Perth, Melbourne and Sydney.

The last chapter of Irish convicts in Australia was written in the adventures of the old whaling ship, *The Catalpa*. She was purchased by American Fenians and, flying the flag of the United States, succeeded in rescuing six Fenians – Thomas Darragh, Martin Hogan, Michael Harrington, Thomas Hasset, Robert Cranston and James Wilson – from Fremantle in April, 1876. The freed prisoners were released in New York in August, having successfully evaded capture by the British naval cutter, *The Georgette*.

The exciting stories of the adventures of the Irish convict political prisoners in Australia would make a dozen epic, action-packed movies! The average Australian with Irish roots today is generally aware that about half of the population has some link with Ireland, and that while only a small percentage of the original convict population were there for political "crimes," the majority of ordinary convicts were being punished for offences which simply reflected the appalling defects of the landlord system which kept ordinary Irish people in hunger and in poverty. Many prisoners, who served their sentences as servants to their masters, became landowners in due course. In the late 1800s, the rush to get rid of as many poor and hungry people as possible resulted in assisted passage schemes taking more than 100,000 emigrants of Irish origin to the new colony, where they worked to repay the cost of their fares. Of these assisted emigrants, the majority came from Cork and Kerry, with counties Clare and Tipperary well to the fore, followed by many Presbyterians from the province of Ulster. Naturally, women were in short supply, and in the new wave of emigration, wives often came out free. The famous Caroline Chisolm devoted her life to encouraging girls to come out and marry in Australia, and she was particularly successful in attracting Irish girls as ideal wives for farmers.

One assisted emigrant girl, Ellen Quinn, from Portadown, County Armagh, married a Kelly from County Tipperary and their son, Ned, became the most notorious and legendary outlaw in Australian history. In folklore he is portrayed as a Robin Hood, who robbed the rich to help the poor but, like the Eureka Stockade diggers, there was an element of "land for the people" and echoes of James Finton Lalor and his teachings in the background. Just like in faraway Tipperary, the Kelly family were on a subsistence farming level, and leant upon both by large ranchers and the forces of law and order. After a fight with the local constabulary, Ned and several companions went on the run and, in a battle with the security forces, shot three policemen. Ned Kelly's famous "armor" of beaten ploughshares, with its almost Norman helmet, spread panic throughout the countryside wherever he appeared, but he and his men came to be regarded as heroes, although they were outlaws on the run for nearly two years. In November, 1880, Ned was captured and hanged in Melbourne Jail. He virtually ran a republic among his own people, and regarded himself as a challenger to their colonial status. His remarkable stance was defended in his own writings and Ned Kelly, despite being an outlaw, holds a very special place in the minds of his countrymen, paradoxically as a figure of justice and freedom. According to his jailers he faced his death quite philosophically and bravely.

The Catholic church in Australia naturally owes an enormous debt to Irish priests, who came from all over Ireland. For example, from the main street of the little town of Cahirciveen in County Kerry came the splendid Irish priest, Father O'Sullivan, who built the Catholic church in Bondi Beach.

Most famous of all Catholic clerics from Ireland was Cardinal Daniel Mannix, Archbishop of Melbourne from 1917 to 1963. He was born in Charleville, in County Cork, and educated at that remarkable seat of learning, St. Colman's College, Fermoy, and then at Maynooth, where he became Professor of Philosophy, of Theology, and finally President. Bishop of Melbourne from 1912, he became Archbishop in 1917, and despite – or perhaps because of his outspokeness – he was made a Cardinal. He was one of the few prelates who had the distinction of being "hove to" by the Royal Navy, off the shores of Ireland, and detained by the authorities. He vigorously denounced the attempt to introduce British conscription to Ireland in World War I, and was equally vehement in condemning the excesses of the Black and Tans and Auxiliary forces in the fight for Independence. On his way to Ireland in 1920, he was arrested and dumped in Penzance, Cornwall, to prevent him from addressing mass meetings in Liverpool, Manchester and Glasgow. He was an ardent Irish Nationalist but opposed to physical force.

Cardinal Daniel Mannix was not the first Prince of the Church in Australia to achieve fame by his championship of the links between his native land and the new world down-under, for one of his predecessors was His Eminence Cardinal Patrick Moran. He was born in 1830, in Leighlinbridge, County Carlow, in the valley of the River Barrow, and was related to the famous Cardinal Cullen of Dublin of the 1860s who so strongly opposed the Fenians. Moran was educated in Rome, became private secretary to his uncle, was ordained a bishop in 1872 and became Archbishop of Sydney in 1884. He plunged into public life in Australia, was very popular with all denominations, and died in Sydney in 1911. Among his many writings were *The Catholics of Ireland under the Penal Laws in the Eighteenth Century* which appeared in a series of papers in *The Australian Catholic Records*, published in Sydney in 1895, and in book form in 1899. A scholar of Hebrew, he was also author of *The Life of Oliver Plunkett* and *Irish Saints in Britain*.

Corkmen, notorious for prospering all over the world by their intellect and charm and skill, did well in Australia. For example, Sir James Martin, born a Fermoy man in 1815, arrived in Sydney with his family at the age of six, and was educated there, becoming a lawyer and a journalist. He entered politics in 1848, became Attorney General, and was Premier in 1863, in 1866 and again in 1870. He was knighted for his public service in 1869, and was buried in Sydney in 1886.

Irish names keep appearing in the limelight of Australia's literary and public life. From Armagh came Victor James Daley, reckoned by many to be one of the leading poets of Australia by virtue of two volumes of his verse published there while he was a journalist. He died in Sydney in 1905. A contemporary of the poet was

Sir Frederick Mathew Darley, a native of Wicklow, who became a lawyer in New South Wales, a member of the legislature, and chief justice in 1886. Before his death in 1910, he had reached the rank of Governor. From Elphin, in County Roscommon, came Roderick Flanagan who founded *The Sydney Chronicle* and edited *The Empire* as well as being the author of *The History of New South Wales,* the province where he died in 1861.

If you look at the map of North Western Australia today, you can see the first gold-mining area of Kimberley. It was discovered by the Irish geologist and surveyor, Edward Townley Hardman, who was born in the town of Drogheda in County Louth, in 1845, and who has a range of mountains named after him in Kimberley. One of Hardman's contemporaries was William Edward Hearn, born in Belturbet in the County of Cavan. Educated at the College of the Holy and Undivided Trinity in Dublin, he became professor of Greek at Queen's University, Galway, and emigrated to Australia to become Dean of the University of Melbourne, where he was also a member of the legislative council of Victoria between 1845 and 1870. Well known for his political and academic works, he died in Melbourne in 1888.

At about this time, Sir Terence Aubrey Murray, a native of Limerick, was a member of the legislature of New South Wales. As a magistrate he had been extremely active in putting down "the wild colonial boys," the bushrangers, who were a headache to established authority. He became Speaker of the House, and was awarded a knighthood in 1869. He was buried in Sydney in 1893, survived by his son, the well-known Professor Gilbert Murray.

Another Irish politician such as Murray was "Big John." Sir John O'Shanassy was born in Thurles, County Tipperary, in 1818. He emigrated to Melbourne in 1839, became a merchant and a banker, and a member of the legislative council alongside his colleague, Sir Charles Gavan Duffy. He died in 1883, a Knight Commander of St. Michael and St. George. Another K.C.M.G. was Sir Arthur Hunter Palmer, born in Armagh, who emigrated to Australia in 1836. He was a farmer who was elected to represent Brisbane in the legislative assembly, and went on to become Premier of Queensland from 1870 to 1874, and Governor of the colony in 1893.

A little while before Palmer, Sir Robert Richard Torrens, born in Cork, emigrated to Australia in 1835, was elected to the Legislative Assembly for Adelaide in 1855, and was made Premier. A lawyer, and graduate of Trinity College, Dublin, he was responsible for the act, which bears his name, which greatly simplified the system of registration of property in Australia. Another legal man of Irish birth was the Honorable Judge Henry Bournes Higgins, born in Newtownards in County Down. He was called to the Victoria Bar and Inner Temple, and became legislative assembly representative for Melbourne. He was a great benefactor to both Irish arts and politics, and died in Melbourne in 1929.

One of the richest men in Australia in his day was Sir Samuel McCaughey, a poor lad from Ballymena in County Antrim, who became the "Sheep King" of Australia, and was knighted in 1903, after a career in parliament. He died in 1919, leaving several million pounds to charities. About the same time, Sir John Henry MacFarland, born in Omagh, in County Tyrone, became master of Ormond College in Melbourne in 1881, and Vice Chancellor of the University of Melbourne in 1910.

Surely the earliest success story of an Irish emigrant to Australia must be that of Andrew Hamilton Hume, who was born in Hillsborough, County Down, in 1762. He emigrated in 1787, and became the founding father of New South Wales. Immensely rich, he died in 1849. His son was one of the first explorers to make his way overland from Sydney to Port Philip. Another early success was D'Arcy Wentworth. Born in Portadown, County Armagh in 1762, he went to New South Wales in 1790, where he became principal surgeon, and built the general hospital in Sydney. His son became a leading politician.

Other politicians of Irish descent include George Higinbotham, born in Dublin in 1826, and John Plunkett, born in Roscommon in 1801. Both were graduates of Trinity College, Dublin, and both were lawyers. Higinbotham edited *The Melbourne Argus* and became a judge, and finally a chief justice. Plunkett became solicitor general for New South Wales, was elected to the legislative assembly, and died in Melbourne in 1869.

As with Irish emigration to the United States of America and to England, it was the custom for brothers and sisters, once established, to send for other members of their families, and frequently those families came from the same counties in Ireland – thus certain townships and cities had heavy concentrations of Mayo people, or people from Clare or Kerry, or what have you. Sydney was a magnet for Irish emigrants, both convicts and free citizens. Free Irish emigrants, in the beginning, naturally drew on Irish convict labor for the development of their holdings and businesses. Boorowa, south of Sydney, became a second Tipperary.

The biggest concentration of Irish descent today is to be found in the eastern states of Queensland, New South Wales, Victoria and, of course, Tasmania. Western Australia comes second on the list, while South Australia has relatively few. Clare men figured prominently in the gold rush, and many an Australian today can boast of a grandfather from a town such as Ennis, County Clare ….

The Irish and New Zealand

To the average Irishman today, New Zealand is best known as the nation which produces the most superb rugby football union touring team in the world, the "All Blacks" and as a very distant country which has always had the friendliest and most understanding relationship with Ireland. The great difference between the New Zealand and the Australian connection with the Emerald Isle is that basically Australia, through a quirk of history, became populated originally by convicts sent out from Britain. That quirk of fate was due to the British loss of the American Colonies, so that the annual supply of convicts who traveled from Britain to work the American plantations came to a standstill, and a new outlet had to be found, and found quickly, for the queueing convicts. So, after 1776, the annual batches of convicts were sent to New South Wales. New Zealand, however, was never a convict settlement and thus its population growth was totally different from that of Australia. It was, indeed, a haven of refuge for escaped convicts from Australia, many of them Irish. Aptly named originally, the "Friendly Islands," and first discovered by the Dutch explorer, Tasman, it fell to Captain Cook, in 1770, to proclaim the region, of which he had made a detailed coast-line survey, a British dominion. At the time, Lord Townshend was in the Vice-Regal seat in Dublin.

As might be expected, the Irish in New Zealand have made their presence felt, mainly in politics, and most of the emigrants were of Presbyterian stock from the province of Ulster. For example, from 1875 onwards, the emigration agent for the northern port of Ireland sent some four thousand Irish settlers to New Zealand. Many of these settled in Tauranga. Most of the early settlers set up their homes all around the coastline of the north and south islands. Among the very first settlers in Wellington were hundreds of Irish origin, and the first Catholic priest there as parish priest was a Father O'Reilly. Similarly, many hundreds of Irish who had come from Australia were among the first citizens of Auckland in the 1840s. With the discovery of gold in the 1860s, Irish miners worked their claims, and then settled in Lake Wakatipu, Kingston and Queenstown.

From the time of the Famine of the 1840s until the time of Gladstone and Parnell in the 1870s, Irish immigrants were few and far between, the majority going to the United States of America, to Canada and to Britain. Under various settlement schemes, about 20,000 Irish immigrants, mainly from the north of Ireland, and mostly laborers, settled in places such as Katikati, a highly organized and successful settlement of Orangemen.

In modern times, Irish emigrants have tended to set out for New Zealand after a period of residence in Britain, and, unlike Irish emigrants to the United States, are largely drawn from the more prosperous counties of the east coast of Ireland.

The political history of New Zealand has seen quite a few prominent individual leaders of Irish origin, such as John Ballance, the leader of the first Liberal Government, who was a native of County Antrim, William Ferguson Massey, the Reform Prime Minister from County Derry, and political leaders such as Fitzgerald, Stafford, Bowen and the Prime Minister Robert Muldoon. The Irish have been more easily assimilated than any other ethnic group in New Zealand, but have cherished their own culture through their schools and churches and Irish societies, and both Hibernian societies and Orange Lodges live in harmony today. The annual St. Patrick's Day feast is well observed by Irishmen with origins in all of the Thirty-Two

Counties of Ireland and leading politicians are always anxious to be seen gracing the various functions celebrating the Wearing of the Green.

One of the most colorful Irish men to make his fortune in New Zealand was Frederick Edward Maning, who was born in County Dublin in 1812, and emigrated to Van Diemen's Land in 1824. He went from there to New Zealand in 1833. At this time Britain was in the process of persuading the Maori tribes to recognize the protection of Britain by buying the land for the Crown from the native tribes. Frederick Maning, an Irishman of enormous charm, strength and sense of humor, was adopted by the natives and made a Maori chief, and he wrote a book on the Maori people. When Britain finally took over the islands they appointed him a judge. He died in London in 1883, by which time the islands of New Zealand were under a Federal Government, with the power of the Maoris broken in their final war of 1860.

Another Irish man successful in negotiating with the Maoris was Sir George Ferguson Bowen, a native of County Donegal. He was Governor of New Zealand in 1867, and was made a Knight Commander of St. Michael and St. George for his services.

Ulstermen usually did well in New Zealand, and one of the most successful was William Massey Ferguson, born in Limavady in 1856, and educated in Derry. He emigrated to New Zealand as a farmer, entered politics in 1870, and was elected to parliament in 1894. He led the opposition for a considerable time and, in 1912, became Prime Minister. He really won the hearts and minds of his people and was Premier during and after the Great War. He was a Privy Councillor, a signatory of the Treaty of Versailles, and a world statesman. He died in Wellington in 1925.

From Queen's County came James Edward Fitzgerald, who was born there in 1818, and who emigrated to New Zealand in 1850. He was one of the founding fathers of Canterbury in South Island, became a member of the first New Zealand parliament, and went on to become Premier in 1854. While in politics he went into journalism and started *The Press* newspaper in 1861.

Comber, County Down, was the birthplace of James McGowan, who emigrated in 1865. He was mayor of Thames, in Auckland, and later Minister of Justice and Mines. A man who accumulated a vast fortune, he became interested in prison reform, and was an authority on the mineral wealth of New Zealand. He died in Thames in 1912.

A Wexford priest, Father Henry William Clery, became Catholic Bishop of Auckland in 1910, and was active in Catholic journalism, editing *The New Zealand Tablet* and founding *The Month*. Like many Catholic clergy he served as a chaplain to the valiant New Zealand forces in the First World War, and was awarded the O.B.E. The Katikati settlement of Orangemen from Ulster was on the northwestern shores of Tauranga Harbor. Like all such settlements, this ten thousand acres of virgin territory was taken from the Maoris. It owed its foundation and success to a very strange character indeed, George Vesey Stewart, who was born in County Tyrone in 1832, and who graduated from Trinity College, Dublin, in 1856. He emigrated to New Zealand in the 1870s. He astutely canvassed the senior landed gentry of his home territory, and tenant farmers drawn from the Orange Lodges, whom he persuaded to emigrate in June, 1875, in a chartered ship carrying thirty-four families of Katikati-bound settlers, and a hundred or so ordinary emigrants. They sailed from Belfast to Auckland – to a land, which if not literally flowing with milk and honey, at least promised that their cattle would be sheltering under their cabbages, and that the minimum size of their potatoes would be that of pumpkins. Vesey Stewart was assisted in his obtaining of land by a fellow graduate of Trinity College, George Maurice O'Rorke, who had preceded him to New Zealand, and had the support of local Irish families, the Sheehans, the Kellys and the Dargavilles. The first settlers were amazingly tenacious, and built up their holdings from swamp lands, fern lands and forest clearings. It was exceedingly hard work – not quite the promised land! – but it succeeded eventually.

The second special group sailed from Belfast in 1878, some 378 of them, and this group included a couple of retired Indian Army generals, a major, a captain or two, a doctor, merchants, and some genteel ladies. They brought money and household goods with them, and had a splendid three-month voyage from Belfast to Auckland. The ex-generals were not to find things quite like the Raj of India, but they all persevered nevertheless.

Vesey Stewart chartered ten ships in all, and brought out five hundred families between 1875 and 1884. When gold was discovered at Waihi, sixteen miles from Katikati, prosperity really came to the settlers. In due course, an Irish Catholic ran the local hotel, and no doubt ensured a supply of "Bushmills" and peace and harmony reigned. When Vesey Stewart died in March, 1920, in his eighties, he had lived to see his settlement scheme grow to a prosperous, pleasant town of several thousand inhabitants. A gallant people, they gave their best in World War I, and some of their number lie in peace in Gallipoli, while others have their names on the Roll of Honor over the Gateway to the battlefields of France. They made their supreme sacrifices again in World War II, in the splendid tradition rooted in Ulster valor.

The Irish and South America

After the defeat of Napoleon and his armies in Europe, thousands upon thousands of soldiers and sailors found themselves demobbed and at a loose end. From 1817 onwards, for a number of years, many Irish volunteers so discharged elected to serve the newly emerging states in South America, such as in the armies of Simon Bolivar in the fight for the freedom of Colombia. Of the thousands who set out for South America, only hundreds arrived, as shipwreck and disease took a heavy toll. Of the hundreds, many were trained seamen, officers and other ranks, who had volunteered for – or had been press-ganged into – the British Navy.

Long before the first arrivistes came to join in the South American wars of freedom from centuries of Spanish oppression, there were famous leaders of Irish stock who had helped put the countries of their adoption on the map.

The most famous of these was Bernardo O'Higgins, a founding father of modern Chile. His father was Don Ambrosio, a Spanish government representative who became Viceroy of Peru. Don Ambrosio was born near Daingean in County Offaly, in 1720, from where he went to Cadiz, and then to Buenos Aires. This remarkable man began his merchant life with a stall in the market place, and eventually became a cavalry captain. He founded the city of San Ambrosio, initiated the highway from Santiago to Valparaiso and also built the city of Osorno. The Spaniards rewarded him for his services by creating him the Marquis of Osorno and, in 1795, Viceroy of Peru. He died in Lima, Peru in 1801. His son, Bernardo O'Higgins, later to become the liberator of Chile, and president of its congress, lived from 1780 to 1846. He was educated initially in Peru, and then in England and Spain, and returned to join the revolutionary movement against the Spanish oppressors. He trained as a soldier, and in a matter of a few years became commander of the army of Chile. Various battles were fought and lost in the mountains of the Andes against superior Spanish forces who were better trained and equipped. Bernardo eventually joined forces with the Argentinian General, San Martin, and together with their armies, they forced the Spaniards out of Chile and captured its capital, Santiago. In 1817 Bernardo was chosen as President of the new republic.

After various battles, during one of which the new President was wounded, the Spanish Royalist forces were finally beaten, and O'Higgins had the unenviable task of putting the nation's affairs in order upon its return to normal civilian life.

To help rid the country and its neighboring coastal nation of Peru of Spanish power, O'Higgins set about founding a navy for Chile. His flagship was called *The O'Higgins* and a Chilean naval force under the command of its first Admiral, Admiral Cochrane, chosen by O'Higgins, went to war to assist Peru against the Spaniards. Simon Bolivar was to become the liberator of Peru, and for a time O'Higgins lived in exile in that country while the affairs of Chile were in chaos. He died on October 23rd, 1842, and lies buried in Santiago. In honor of this Irish liberator, the main street in Santiago is called after O'Higgins, a permanent reminder of Irish-South American links.

Another great contributor to the freedom from Spain of the South American Republics was Admiral William Brown, founder of the Argentinian Navy. He was born in Foxford, County Mayo, on June 23rd, 1777. He emigrated to America with his family when he was nine years old and, at the age of nineteen, after some years at sea, he was press-ganged into the British Navy. He finished up as a captain in command of a British merchant ship, a cabin-boy-to-captain story.

Captain William Brown arrived with his family in Buenos Aires in 1812. At this time, the revolutionary leaders of Buenos Aires were at war with Spain and, recognizing the abilities of Brown, they offered him the command of the navy of the United Provinces, who were seeking freedom. Together with another captain from Ireland, he put together quite a formidable little fleet of merchant ships converted to warships, and a third Irishman, John Santiago King, assisted in the command. Brown went to war attacking the Spaniards, their supply ships and their land batteries. One of the ships under his command was *The Belfast*. Off Montevideo, Uruguay, he defeated a superior force of Spanish ships and smashed the sea power of Spain. Montevideo was then captured, its Spanish warships, merchant ships and military stores seized, and the struggle for the independence of Chile was furthered greatly.

After his famous victory of Montevideo, Brown headed round the Horn to harass Spanish sea and land forces, blockading ports and capturing enemy shipping. He retired from the sea only to return to fight as Admiral of a new fleet against the aggressor, Brazil. He broke the Brazilian blockade of Buenos Aires from 1826 to1827 and was later wounded in action. He acted as governor of Buenos Aires, and in the 1840s, for the third time, he commanded the Argentine fleet during an outbreak of civil war, blockading Montevideo from 1842 to 1845, and then retired to live in his beloved city. He died at his modest property there on May 3rd, 1857.

The links between Ireland and South America have frequently been forged through soldiers or sailors of fortune offering their services to the emergent South American republics, and yet there have been many links in peacetime. In our time there are many individual Irish missionaries who have volunteered to devote their lives to work among the poor and oppressed in the slums of South American capital cities, and in remote rural areas, where the peasantry are under constant threat of starvation, or worse, laboring under oppressive military regimes. In the years following World War II, the lead was given to newly ordained priests in Cork to go out to serve the poor of South America by the Reverend Archdeacon Canon Duggan of Cork, who was later to die in the South American mission field at the age of seventy-five.

Many purely commercial links were forged by the men and women of County Meath who went out to South America, notably to the Argentine, because of their expert knowledge of cattle and cattle breeding. William Bulfin, in his work *Rambles in Erin*, first published in 1907, about his three-thousand-mile cycle ride throughout the length and breadth of Ireland, recalls the ties between Buenos Aires and Mullingar. On the road to the great cattle town of Mullingar he says: "I was told by a truthful man up the road that one could not see a soul in this part of the country who has not a relation in Argentina." When the local people heard he had been in Buenos Aires, they crowded around him: "I stayed with them for more than two hours. A few of them remembered their Spanish and plied me with it. There were brothers and sisters of men I had met on the pampas, and nieces and nephews and even parents as well." Bulfin had emigrated to Argentina from Galway at the age of seventeen, and had worked as a range hand on the pampas. He became a journalist and edited *The Southern Cross* of Buenos Aires. He returned to Ireland in 1902.

South America was a haven of refuge for John Devereux, who fought in the Irish Wexford Rising of 1798, was taken prisoner, and was allowed to go to France. Napoleon offered to create him a general, but he declined, and formed an Irish Brigade, which served in Simon Bolivar's Army of Independence. In his time he was known as the "Lafayette of South America," and became a general in the army of Venezuela.

Simon Bolivar's aide-de-camp and personal secretary was Daniel Florence O'Leary, who was born in Cork in 1800. He joined a regiment of hussars and fought in the Bolivian War of Independence. He was made minister for Peru for his services, to Brazil, Chile and the Central States of America. He died in Bogota in 1877.

While Irishmen fought in South America in support of the new Republics against the old Imperial order of Spain, and fought on both sides of the American Civil War, one of the strangest battles ever fought by Irishmen was in the service of Mexico, against the "Imperial" might of the United States of America. This was in 1847, before Mexico found oil and earned the respect of her northern neighbor. Today, because of an educational system which owes much to the Irish Christian Brothers, many Mexicans are aware of Ireland and her history and every year, on the feast of Saint Patrick, they pay tribute, in Mexico City, to the "memory of the Irish soldiers of the heroic Saint Patrick's Battalion, martyrs who gave their lives for the cause of Mexico during the unjust North American invasion of 1847." It is a curious story, and a plaque on the wall in the Plaza San Jacinto, a suburb of Mexico City, names seventy-one Irishmen of the Mexican Saint Patrick's Battalion who were either hanged or imprisoned by the invading United States Army. The names are there for all to read: "O'Reilly, Hanly, Sheehan, Hogan, Delaney, O'Connor, Nolan, Dalton, Fitzpatrick, Casey, McDowell, Cavanaugh, Cassidy, Daly, Kelly, Murphy ...." More than 50 were to die by the old-fashioned hangman's rope of the United States Army.

The United States Army sat on the Rio Grande facing the army of Mexico. Of the thousands of troops encamped, half were immigrants, and almost five hundred were Irish, and Catholic at that. The Mexican priests assiduously worked on this fact during the months of waiting, and their propaganda war was highly successful, as several hundred American soldiers, mostly raw Catholic country boys from Ireland, were persuaded to cross the Rio Grande and form the "San Patricio" battalion, with their own green flag, in the Mexican Army! Captain John O'Reilly was their leader, and the battalion, like the Lincoln Brigade almost a century later in the service of the Spanish Republic, fought for "democracy," this time alongside the Mexicans against the United States' forces in 1846 and 1847. The day of reckoning came to these men in the final push by the United States Army for Mexico City. Enormously superior American forces led by men whom were later to become generals of the American Civil War, swept down on the Mexican Army, and at the strong point of Churubusco Convent, the Saint Patrick's battalion, with their artillery, held out for a considerable time.

The Mexicans lost thousands in the battle, the Americans a few hundred. The Irish men in Mexican uniforms were overwhelmed, and all but seventy one were killed or taken prisoner. Twenty were immediately court-martialed as deserters and hanged on September 10th, 1847, and more than that number were subsequently hanged, *en masse*, as "Old Glory" finally flew victoriously over the remains of the last castle which had been defended to the death by young Mexican officer cadets. It was not a victory to be sung from the rooftops, or gloried in a film featuring the dashing John Wayne.... It was a case of homesick, illiterate country boys deserting an "Imperial" fighting machine for a romantic and lost cause, the people – Mexican and Irish peasants – versus the generals.

Ireland and the Continent

At first glance, Ireland, as an offshore island off an offshore island on the edge of the Atlantic Ocean, remote, romantic and untrodden by the Roman legions, does not appear to be in the mainstream of Europe. However, from the earliest of pre-Christian times, the dividing seas around her have been her connecting sea roads – the equivalent of today's motorways and autobahns, linking her closely not only with Scotland, Wales and England, but with France, Spain, Portugal, Germany, Austria, Italy and even with Russia.

The early pagan Celts, particularly during the time of the collapse of the Roman Empire, poured down through the Irish Sea and the Channel in enormous fleets of pirate ships, sweeping up thousands of prisoners as slaves – including one from the Severn Estuary who was destined to return as Saint Patrick, the Evangelist of Ireland. These Celtic warriors, who flung themselves almost naked into battle, armed only with a short, stabbing sword, have been aptly described by the Roman historian, Diodorus Siculus, writing one hundred years before the birth of Christ:

"Physically the Celts are terrifying in appearance, with deep-sounding and very harsh voices. In conversation they use few words and speak in riddles, for the most part hinting at things and leaving a great deal to be understood. They frequently exaggerate with the aim of extolling themselves and diminishing the status of others. They are boasters and threateners, and given to bombastic self-dramatization, and yet they are quick of mind and with good natural ability for learning."

In fact their natural ability for learning was such that they became intoxicated with the message of Christianity brought to them by Saint Patrick in the year 432 AD, and the whole nation burst forth between the fifth and the ninth centuries in monastic universities, centers of learning which kept the light of Christ aglow in Ireland during the Dark Ages. These monks returned in vast numbers as "peregrini" – wanderers for the sake of Christ – who spread throughout Europe as far as Kiev in Russia. Staff in hand, wearing a roughspun habit and cowl with a rope cord tied at the waist and shod with sandals, they favored the "half-corona" hairstyle, the hair tonsured right across the front of the head, and they must have looked somewhat eccentric to pagan Europe. They carried no material possessions with them and brought civilization – Latin, Greek and Christianity – back through Europe, leading them by the scholar's hand and the sound of the Mass bell. They set up their stalls at the court of the Emperor Charlemagne and shouted "knowledge for sale!"

Saint Colmcille set up his monastery-university in Iona in 563 AD, and evangelized the Scots. Saint Aidan took on the English in 635 AD, and Saint Finian tackled the Welsh. Saint Columbanus, from Bandor, spread his rule of life like a fire throughout France, founding the Monastery of Luxeuil in 590 AD, and Annegray and Fontaines. His rule of life was so successful, and so widespread, that it rivaled the classic Benedictine rule. Eventually, because it was so austere, it gave way to the popularity of the "Pax" of the Benedictines, who brought tranquility out of chaos by leading people back to cultivate the land and to lead a quiet, spiritual life. Saints Fiacre and Kilian settled in Meaux and Aubiguy, while Saint Fursey founded the Monastery of Lagny, anpPalace of Charles the Bald, while other Irish monks set up in Rheims, Metz and Ghent. Liege fell under the influence of Irish monk scholars, as did Aix La Chapelle, Pavia, Cologne and Mainz. Ratisbon, Wurzburg and Mecklenburg too fell to the learning of the "peregrini."

Peronne can, perhaps, be taken as a symbol of the different ways in which the cultures of two contrasting European nations, such as Ireland and Germany, can sweep into the cultural stream of a third nation, in this instance France, and make vastly differing historical contributions in different centuries.

Gerard Manley Hopkins, Victorian writer and Jesuit priest, once described Luther as the "Wild Beast of the Waste Wood," and his Prussian spiritual descendants, such as Hitler's Panzer General, Heinz Guderian, made Peronne their headquarters in World War II, when they blitzed their way to the Channel Ports in 1940. This ex-cavalry officer of World War I, who had fought on the Somme and the Aisne, wrote in his memoirs "Tanks are a life-saving weapon." To many Germans, Peronne spells tank warfare country, where the ex-butcher, SS Panzer leader Sepp Dietrich, ripped his way through Pilgrimage country to the great joy of his fellow generals, Von Runstedt and Von Kleist.

To the Irish pilgrims, Peronne is just down the road from the first retreat of yet another Irish saint, Saint Gobain; while Laon, perched three hundred feet above the rolling plains, was a hive of ninth century Irish scholarship and Soissons embarrassingly full of Irish monks, as were Cambrai and Rheims in the seventh, eighth and ninth centuries.

France really deserves a mammoth chapter to herself for her Irish connections. The first "invasion" was by Irish monks during the seventh through the ninth centuries, who strode through the French countryside bringing back Christianity to the pagan Gauls. The second wave of "invasion" brought scholarship and the arts with Christianity and the third wave was made up of pilgrims on their way to the famous shrines of France and Rome, to that of Saint James of Compostela in Spain, and as far as Jerusalem itself.

Saint Patrick knew Tours and Lyons, where he studied for many years, and his disciples, more than fifty of them, evangelized Brittany and all of northern France. Not all of these saints were men – two of the women, for example, were Irish princesses – Saint Osnamme, whose bones are preserved in the little village of Fericy in the Seine-et-Marne district, and Saint Ozanne of Jouarre. The Champagne country today still venerates the relics of Irish saints Gibrien and Tresain.

These were "little" or lesser known saints, and for "star quality" one looks to the two archbishops of Armagh who died while on pilgrimage in France, the most famous saint of all being Saint Malachy, who died in the arms of Saint Bernard of Clairvaux, in Burgundy.

Irish pilgrims, in the course of history, were duly replaced by young men who trained for the priesthood in France, when persecution forbade such schools of learning in their native Ireland. For centuries, half of the priests of Ireland were trained in the Irish college in Paris – founded in 1578 in Nantes – and in seminaries in other cities. Small wonder that today the people of France feel so much at home as tourists in Ireland, and similarly, the Irish in France feel not only close to the French people, but can conjure up ghosts and visions of many an Irish saint and scholar who has trodden the same roads before them through the glorious French countryside and the majestic cathedral cities.

There are all too few books on Irish swordsmen in the service of France, or on the part played by Irishmen and women in the French Revolution, or the last invasion of Ireland by the French, when the province of Connaught rose against the redcoats in 1798. France has been a friend to insurgent Ireland since the days of Henry III of France, who tried to assist the rebellion of the province of Munster in the fight against the forces of the English Virgin Queen in 1572.

The France of 1688 provided military advisers, troops and officers to James II in his fight against William of Orange. James ran from the Battle of the Boyne in indecent haste (with a nosebleed recorded in Arklow), before he fled in disgrace back to France. His name has gone down in Gaelic history as "Seamus the Shite!" Strange to relate, the Vatican sent up a fervent "Te Deum" for the Protestant William of Orange on his victory at the Boyne over Catholic James.

The French Revolution had a profound effect on the movement known as the United Irishmen, founded by Theobald Wolfe Tone, which endeavored to unite Irish Presbyterian and Catholic in a form of republicanism.

In Irish history, 1798 was "the Year of the French," as it was then that they landed a military expeditionary force in the Bay of Killala in County Mayo. It was defeated, and while French officers and troops were spared as prisoners of war, the Irish rebel peasantry and their French-trained Irish leaders, were massacred by the redcoats and German mercenary troops, the Hessians. The Hessians behaved in Ireland as did many of their descendants in the German invasion of Poland in World War II. When the rising of Connaught had been finally crushed, French ships once again sailed into Killala Bay but, being too late to be of any help, they quietly returned to France. In Lough Swilly, off the coast of Donegal, the ship carrying Theobald Wolfe Tone was taken, and he was imprisoned in Dublin where he died in mysterious circumstances, a death said by his captors to have been suicide.

The Irish struggle for freedom continued, largely with the aid of the French. It was the French who helped inspire the insurrection of 1848, and it was in France that the Fenians – the Irish Republican Brotherhood – first learned their trade, and became heavily influenced by the French revolutionary philosophy of violence, anti-clericism and the destruction of religious education in schools – aspects of the less acceptable face of modern anarchical revolution.

The Sheehys – the original clan of Gallowglasses – were gentlemen from twelfth-century Scotland who hired out their double-headed battle-axes as bodyguards to Irish kings and princes. They fared well in exile in France. Mostly from the province of Munster and the counties of Kerry and Limerick, they provided a medical consultant to the French royal court in the person of Doctor John Sheehy. The Revolution saw Bernard Sheehy involved in the French Expedition to Ireland in 1796. He was a military adviser and assistant to General Wolfe Tone and was later singled out by Napoleon Bonaparte as his aide-de-camp. He was killed in action by Napoleon's side on February 8th, 1807, in the Battle of Eylau during the first encounter of the French armies with the Russians.

Austria has had a special fascination for the wandering Irish since the monks of the ninth century. Ever chivalrous, when the militant Prussian, Frederick the Great, declared war on Maria Theresa of Austria, Irishmen flocked to her aid and joined her regular army, so much so, that at one time there were no less than thirty Irish generals in the Imperial Army. The best-known descendants of these generals were Brownes, Fitzgeralds, Nugents, O'Donnells, O'Connells, Lacys, O'Briens and Taaffes and, in 1915, Viscount Taaffe was Field Marshal, Minister of State and Chamberlain to the Emperor Franz Joseph.

As early as 1620, Thomas Carve, born in Tipperary in 1590, was the Catholic chaplain to the Austrian Foreign Legion. Francis MacDonnell, born in Connaught in 1656, joined the Austrian Army and captured the French Marshal Villeroi in battle. Count Andrew O'Reilly, who was born in Ireland in 1742, distinguished himself in the Seven Years War, fought at the battles of Amberg and

Ulm in 1796, as well as at Kehl, and was made Governor of Vienna, the city where he died in 1832. His fellow Irish soldier, Field Marshal Brady, started life as a theological student destined for the priesthood in Vienna, and gave this up to enter the army of Maria Theresa. Field Marshal Nugent left Austria for England in 1811 and became diplomatic representative for his adopted country.

Many other Irishmen achieved eminence and it is probable that many Austrian citizens today, particularly in Vienna, who bear Irish names are unaware of their ancestral connections with the Emerald Isle.

Nobody who has strolled the Viennese streets and palaces and the vast official buildings of the Austro-Hungarian Emperor, Franz Joseph, can have anything but sympathy for his young and beautiful wife, the Empress Elizabeth, who always longed for the freedom to hunt with horse and hound. To her great joy, in the 1860s she was able to hunt in Ireland, where she set up households in County Meath. On one famous occasion, while out hunting, she cleared the high wall of the all-male bastion of the Catholic priests of Ireland, Maynooth College in County Kildare. Such was her charm that the President of the College invited her to a solemn High Mass in the seminary's chapel. Thus the training ground for many Irish priests, financed by the British government – a cold, damp, haunted, masculine establishment – was to receive in due course, a generous gift in return for their grave but friendly reception. It took the form of an enormous and gorgeous statue, in solid silver, of Saint George and the Dragon, which can still be seen today by visitors to Maynooth. The Empress obviously saw little difference between the contemporary England of Victoria and the rather British outpost in Maynooth, and mistook Saint George for the patron saint of Ireland. In addition, the beautiful wife of the last of the powerful Hapsburgs gave the College Fathers an expensive and elaborate gift of a set of mass vestments, which can also be seen by today's visitors. The Empress Elizabeth was undoubtedly the most beautiful huntress ever to grace the Ward Union and the Meath hounds in Ireland. The happiest days of her life were spent in Ireland, and she was much loved by the ordinary people who appreciated both her beauty and her skill as a horsewoman.

Switzerland saw the site of the Monastery of Saint Gall, on the spot which now bears his name. Saint Fergal, who became known as Saint "Vergilius," set up in Salzburg, and Austria's most illustrious martyr was Saint Colman, from Cork, whose tomb can be seen today at the Benedictine Abbey of Melk. Italy saw Saint Fridian set himself up at Lucca, and Donatus at Fiesole and Saint Cathaldus at Taranto.

Not all the Irish wanderers were monks and saints. For example, the oldest clan in Europe is the Clan O'Neill, which goes back to the sixth century and whose titular chief, "Prince and Count of Tyrone," now resides near Lisbon in Portugal and is a kinsman of that noble lord, Raymond O'Neill, resident at Shane's Castle, County Antrim.

Another big Irish invasion of Europe came as the forces of the Virgin Queen, Elizabeth I, smashed up the old Gaelic order in Ireland and forced its aristocratic leaders to flee abroad in defeat and exile. This became known as the "Flight of the Earls," when the princely O'Donnells and the O'Neills sailed for Spain. Later, as the Williamite forces defeated the Irish at the Battle of the Boyne in 1690, and at Limerick in 1691, ten thousand officers and men sailed into exile and formed Irish brigades in the armies of the Continent. These were known as the "Wild Geese." As Thomas Davis, the poet of *The Nation* tells us:

"The recruiting for the Brigade was carried on in the French Ships which smuggled brandies, wines and silks, etc., to the western and south-western coasts. Their return cargoes were recruits for the Brigade, and were entered in their books as 'Wild Geese.' Hence this became the common name in Ireland for the Irish serving in the Brigade. The recruiting was chiefly from Clare, Limerick, Kerry and Galway."

General Patrick Sarsfield, the hero of the battle for Limerick, was killed on July 29th, 1693, at the Battle of Landen, leading his troops to victory against the Williamite forces. As he lay dying in the midst of a great victory he said, "Oh! that this were for Ireland," summing up the sentiments of the "Wild Geese" fighting the Saxon and other foes in Europe.

The songs, ballads and poems of this period of glamorous Irish history, including the celebration of the famous victory of Fontenoy in 1745, were all very well, but they overlooked the plight of the leaderless mass of people left behind in Ireland. All that the lone freedom fighter could do was to live the life of a hunted "rapparee," and sally forth occasionally to strike a blow for freedom from the mountains of Wicklow, from the Glen of Aherlow, from the limestone caves of the Burren of Clare or the valleys and woodlands of Donegal, until he was hunted down to be hanged, or killed in battle by the occupying forces.

Many of the Irish leaders trained in the fencing schools of France and became the greatest swordsmen of their day. Several returned to Galway and enjoyed the thrill of challenging the Williamite usurpers of their land to a gentleman's duel. The Williamites were not skilled in swordplay, and thus many leading families were deprived prematurely of their arrogant young sons. Due to the inequality of skills in swordplay, the first rules of dueling were set up in Galway – pistols at dawn at twenty paces. This evened up the chances of survival for the young Williamite bloods in their duels with their French-trained opponents. Voltaire, commenting on the military genius of the Irish in the service of France, admired their gallantry fighting abroad and said that they had "always fought badly at home." This was echoed by Thomas Davis, who commented that the "Wild Geese" fought with all the advantages of French discipline and equipment, and as soldiers with the rights of war, and not as "Rebels, with halters round their necks."

The Green Flags of the Irish Brigades on the Continent

soon carried the battle honors of Cremona, Spire, Luzzara, Blenheim, Cassano, Ramillies, Almanza, Alcira, Malplaquet and Denain. The second Irish Brigade formed in France assisted Vauban to victory at the siege of Namur, a battle which was fought with over 100,000 troops on either side. Irish cavalry fought valiantly in Italy; in 1702 the regiments of Dillon and Burke rescued the city of Cremona, the troops turning out in their shirts at night, awakened by the sound of invading horsemen. The Imperial Cuirassiers of Baron Freiberg were repulsed in a bloody triumph which all Europe applauded. A year later, Nugent's regiment of horsemen were to cut up the German cavalry of the Prince of Hesse. At the Battle of Ramillies in 1706, Clare's Dragoons cut through and seized the English colors, the standard of the veteran Coldstream Guards.

When Dillon and his regiment fought at Barcelona, a twelve-year-old boy, son of a Galway man, fought alongside him – he was later to become Count Lally de Tollendal, who came to be renowned for his service with the French in India.

It was after the news of the defeat of the Duke of Cumberland at Fontenoy by the famous bayonet charge of the Irish regiments that King George II is reputed to have said of the Penal Code, "Cursed be the laws which deprive me of such subjects."

The names of Irish Officers appear today in honor on the Arc de Triomphe in Paris and, in the opening words of his essay, *The Irish Brigade*, Thomas Davis observed: "When valour becomes a reproach, when patriotism is thought a prejudice, and when a soldier's sword is a sign of shame, the Irish Brigade will be forgotten or despised."

The Irish were loath to stay out of European wars – some 250,000 served in the British forces in World War I. They, like many, died bloodily in their thousands, and Professor Tom Kettle, an Irish Volunteer, summed up their thoughts when he wrote the following lines a few days before he was killed on the Western Front:

"So here, while the mad guns curse overhead
And tired men sigh with mud for couch and floor,
Know that we fools, now with the foolish dead,
Died not for Flag, nor Emperor,
But for a dream, born in a herdsman's shed,
And for a secret scripture of the poor."

It is probable that, between the 1600s and the 1800s, up to three quarters of a million Irishmen fought and died in Continental wars, starting with the first 30,000 members of the Irish Brigades who served under Louis XIV. The names of the Irish generals are like a roll call of the most famous clans in Irish history and include Dillon, O'Mahony, Butler, O'Farrell, Dunsany, O'Gara, O'Donnell, McCarthy, O'Neill, Burke, Barry and Murphy. Some reached the greatest heights as, for example, Marshal Patrick McMahon, who became President of the Republic of France. O'Donnells became generals and field marshals in the service of Austria, as did Lacys, Brownes and Nugents. Field Marshal Count

Taaffe, from Sligo, fought with his regiment for Austria. Spain was served by Field Marshal Count Alexander O'Reilly, from County Meath, who led his Irish Brigade of the Regiments of Hibernia, Irlanda and Ultonia (Ulster). It gave rise to the flag of the latter regiment being named Gerona after the victory they won in the city of that name in Catalonia against the invading forces of Napoleon. As a result, a Spanish infantry regiment became known as "Irlanda el Famosa" and Count O'Reilly became Captain General of Andalusia.

To capture something of the extraordinary history of the Irish, and their historical connections with continental Europe down through the ages, it is worth visiting the ancestral home of the O'Conor Don, at Clonalis House in Castlerea, County Roscommon. The O'Conor Don is a direct descendant of the last High King of Ireland, Turlough Mor O'Conor, who died in 1156. In the portrait gallery at Clonalis House today, you can see the faces of this family of such continental significance. There is Major Owen O'Conor, Count and Countess O'Rourke, and Don Carlos O'Conor. Count O'Rourke, father of Bishop O'Rourke, was killed fighting against Marlborough at the Battle of Luzzara. His wife was maid-of-honor at King James' court in France. The O'Conors fought as brigadiers and officers in the service of France, particularly in the regiment of Dillon. In the dining room is a portrait of Don Carlos O'Conor, diplomat of Spain. The O'Conors had links with South America, and also with the United States of America. The portrait of Charles O'Conor of New York shows the first Catholic ever to be nominated to the Presidency of the United States. Clonalis House has one of the finest private collections of books and historical family papers in Ireland, and the Clan O'Conor, spread literally throughout the world, has historical records spanning nine hundred years and more. The survival of such a family reflects the history of a people who kept their faith and ancient heritage, despite all adversity. By all the laws, the Clan O'Conor, and the whole Irish race, should be extinct. But they have survived, largely because it is the nation which can endure the most, rather than that which inflicts the most, which lives on in history.

Irish Roots

If a person is of Irish descent and wishes to trace his ancestors, it can be a lot of fun, and quite often it ends in success – although the odds are very much against finding all there is to know in many cases! In the first place, it is handy to know from which of the Thirty-Two Counties the ancestors came, bearing in mind that Queen's County is now called County Laois; King's County, County Offaly; Queenstown is now Cobh; and Kingstown, Dun Laoghaire – to name but a few. The county of origin on both parental sides should ideally be established, along with the correct spelling of the surname, since often an "O" or a "Mac" becomes lost on emigration. Christian names are helpful, as the custom has largely been to pass down a father's christian name to his son. With the surname, christian name and county of origin, it is useful to glean from family folklore, word of mouth, old letters, old deeds, or inscriptions in old books, from what parish or town the ancestors came. If a family can remember a parish or a townland, then half the quest is over. It is helpful to know if the relations were farmers, shopkeepers or professional people; and their religion, be it Catholic, Church of Ireland, Presbyterian or Quaker, as each has its own records. The most difficult tracings are, of course, from the mass emigration of the famine years from 1845 onwards. But it is still possible to do a trace in many cases.

In Ireland, the registration of births, marriages and deaths began in 1864, and records are kept at the offices of the Registrar-General at the Custom House in Dublin. Non-Catholic marriages are recorded here from 1845. The Public Record Office in the Four Courts, Dublin, holds many tithe payment records, and all manner of records relating to wills. The Registry of Deeds office, Henrietta Street, Dublin, has property information dating from the 1700s.

The National Library in Kildare Street, Dublin, has one of the best-informed, most patient and diligent library staffs in the whole ancestor-tracing world. Here are directories, antiquarian journals, family histories, and vast collections of national and local newspapers in which to delve.

If the ancestor was of the Catholic faith, then once a parish or a townland of origin has been established, a visit can be paid to the parochial registers of the local Catholic parish church in Ireland, where most parish priests are of considerable help, understanding and patience in the game of "roots."

In the "Twenty-Six" counties there are, alas, considerable gaps in many public records, as in the turbulent days of the fight for freedom, and in the subsequent Civil War, hundreds of thousands of public records were blown sky-high, or burnt to the ground. In the "Six Counties" however, the Public Record Office in Belfast has excellent records, particularly of tithes and their payments.

Tombstone hunting has its place in ancestor tracing, but the mass of unmarked graves of famine victims, or families frequently too poor to erect inscribed stones, rather limits this field of interest. The ancestors would need to have been wealthy indeed to have had family tombs!

Despite the difficulties which can be encountered, it is still well worth the attempt to trace ones ancestors, even though that attempted trace may be unsuccessful, since in the process something will be learned of the time and place of leaving the original homestead, and this helps to illuminate the history of the dispersal of a restless people all over the known world.

A five-story round tower (previous page), 103 feet tall and fifty-two feet in circumference, still stands straight and relatively undamaged after more than 1,000 years as part of the now ruined monastery of Glendalough, County Wicklow. These arrow-like towers were not easily accessible; the entrance was usually five meters up the shaft, and reachable only by ladder. They often served as lookouts and bell towers to warn against Viking raids, and monks and manuscripts survived attacks by sheltering in them. Saint Kevin lived a hermit's live in Glendalough, often sheltering in the hollows of trees, and dying here in 618. The glen itself takes its name from the Irish Gleann Dá Loch – the Valley of Two Lakes. Left: the Vale of Clara, County Wicklow, and (overleaf) the mountainous Cooley Peninsula, County Louth.

The Bank of Ireland (above), Dublin, was begun in 1729 by Sir Edward Lovett Pearce to house the Irish Parliament – a purpose rendered redundant by the 1800 Act of Union. The Easter Rising of 1916 from the O'Connell Street General Post Office, Dublin, resulted in much of the street's east side being destroyed. Bullets even chipped at John Henry Foley's statue of Daniel O'Connell (right and overleaf), "The Liberator," which stands on the north side of O'Connell Bridge.

The Metal Footbridge, etched out in solid black lines against a Dublin evening, spans the dark waters of the River Liffey. The name Dublin comes from two Irish words, Dubh Linn, meaning "dark pool" and describing the Liffey. The city is still known to Gaelic-speaking Irish by an ancient reference to its river: Baile Atha Cliath, "the town of the hurdle ford." However, Dublin was not founded by the Irish at all, but by the Danish. These Scandinavians, perhaps history's greatest seafarers, seem to have agreed with the Greek geographer Ptolemy, who mentioned the site as a place of note, and they took advantage of its favorable position to form a settlement. Dublin remained Danish until the Battle of Clontarf on Good Friday, 1014, when the Irish chieftain Brian Boru led his forces to victory.

Above: the Long Room of Trinity College (these pages), Dublin. This high-vaulted, first-floor room houses the Old Library and its special displays. Among the many treasures owned by Trinity College Library are four Shakespeare folios and the Book of Kells, illuminated in the sixth century by monks using inks made according to a secret process. A leaf of the book is turned daily. Trinity was established in 1591 on the site of the former Priory of All Hallows and distinguished itself by admitting women as early as 1903.

The 1890 National Museum (facing page bottom), Dublin, contains articles as diverse as the eighth-century Tara brooch and the harp of Turlough O'Carolan, as well as Irish nationalist exhibits from the 1916 Rising, James Connolly's blood-stained shirt and the barrister Pearse's wig and gown among them. Facing the National Museum and also designed by Sir Thomas Newenham Deane and his son, the National Library (facing page top) was founded in 1877 for the Royal Dublin Society. The National Gallery of Ireland (above) stands in Leinster Lawn, Merrion Square, and was opened in 1864. It seems to have been dedicated to the spirit of George Bernard Shaw's words: "I believe in Michelangelo, Velasquez, and Rembrandt; in the might of design, the mystery of color, the redemption of all things by Beauty everlasting, and the message of Art that has made these hands blessed."

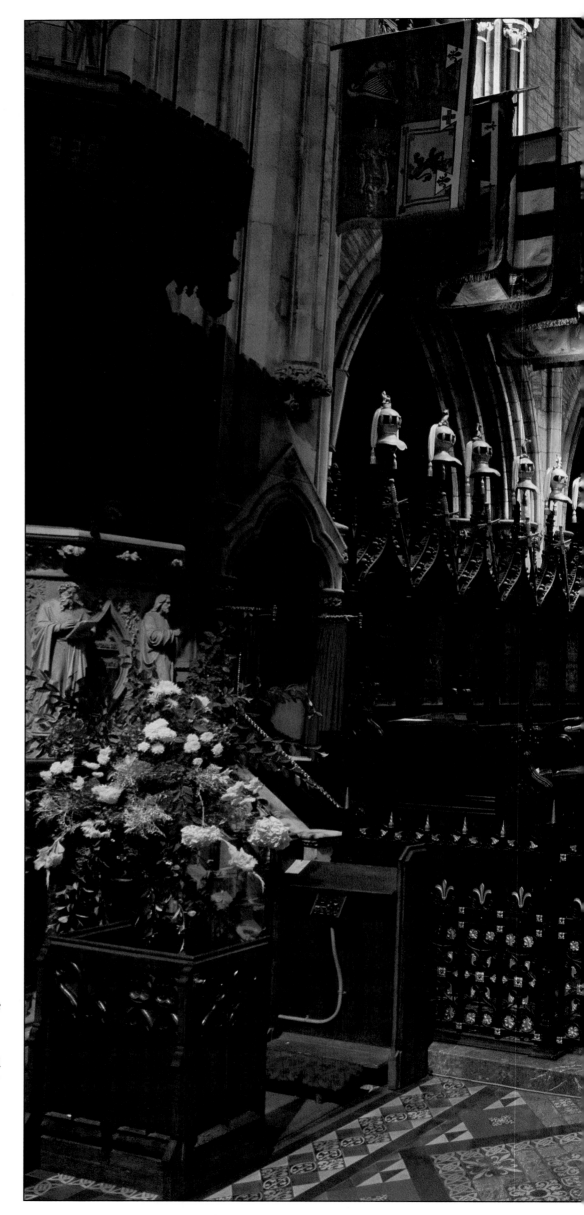

The choir and sanctuary of St. Patrick's Cathedral. Tradition holds that Saint Patrick baptized converts in a well on a small island upon which St. Patrick's Cathedral now stands. The well was discovered in 1901 during excavations and is preserved in the northwest end of the Cathedral. St. Patrick's was founded around 1190 to counter the influence of nearby Christ Church Cathedral. St. Patrick's most famous dean, Jonathan Swift, whose satirical tale Gulliver's Travels *every schoolchild knows, is buried in the south aisle, near the tomb of Esther Johnson. She was "Stella," one of Swift's two great loves. His self-composed epitaph reads:* Ubi saeva indignatio ulteris cor lacerare nequit – *"He lies where fierce indignation can no longer rend his heart."*

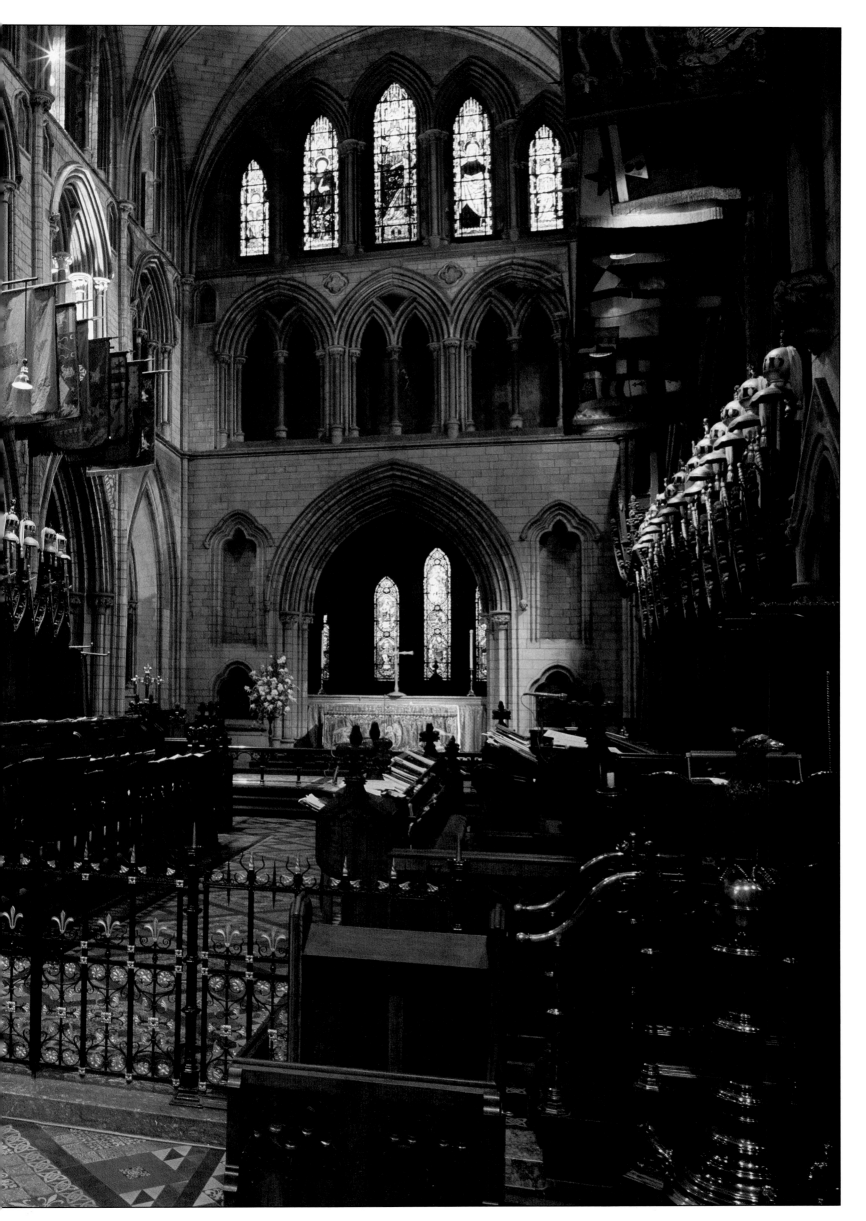

The National Gallery of Ireland owns many famous works from a wide variety of schools, including work by Michelangelo. Its exhibits include the Andrew O'Connor plaster model (above) for his statue of General Lafayette, and a copy of Giovanni Piamontini's marble The Wrestlers *(right), the original of which stands in the Uffizi Gallery, Florence. On the southern side of Dublin Castle, magnificent Waterford crystal chandeliers are suspended above the French silk upholstery in the State Drawing Room (top right) of the State Apartments, which were home to the English viceroys. In the middle of the room stands a thirteenth-century Chinese punchbowl adorned with wedding scenes.*

Many of Ireland's greatest wordsmiths have been moved to write about Dublin's streets (these pages). This city, which retains many of its historical frontages, now carefully preserved, was described ambivalently by McNeice: "With her seedy elegance /With her gentle veils of rain /And all that hide behind /Her Georgian façades" (above).

Phoenix Park (above and top left), Dublin, was enclosed by the Duke of Ormonde in 1671 on land confiscated from the Knights Hospitallers at Kilmainham. Its name comes from fionn uisce, *meaning "clear water," in reference to a spring which is now in the grounds of the zoo. South of the River Liffey, the Grand Canal (left) forms an arc, running from the west of Dublin to the Grand Canal Docks in the east.*

Cahir, or Cathair Dhuin Lascaigh, *meaning*
"Fortress of the Fish Abounding," is dominated
by a castle standing on a rocky island in the
River Suir. Extensively restored in 1840, the
castle was probably begun in the twelfth century,
but today its dominant features are the sturdy
fortifications dating from the fifteenth century.
Cahir was the Tipperary seat of a branch of the
Butler family, the branch that did not convert
and join the English forces. The castle was
therefore besieged by the Earl of Essex in 1599.
In a rare success, Essex captured the castle
within a few days. Cromwell also seized it, in
1650, on his way to capture the town of Clonmel.
The remarkable completeness of the Cahir's keep
and walls is due to a lack of extreme defiance on
the part of its past inhabitants. It was opened to
the public in 1971.

Ardmore's ninety-seven-foot-high round tower (above) in County Waterford dates from the twelfth century and was one of the last of its type to be built. It has four storys, and projecting stones on the interior have been carved into grotesque heads. The ruined "cathedral" beside it was the thirteenth-century St. Declan's Church. Right: Waterford, on the banks of the River Suir. Cashel (top right), famous for its cathedral, Cormac's Chapel, round tower and the Cross of Cashel, stands out from the plain of Tipperary and is the spot where, in A.D. 450, St. Patrick baptized King Aengus.

Kinsale Harbor, County Cork (these pages and overleaf), lies at the foot of Compass Hill on the estuary of the River Bandon and is appropriately named from the Irish Ceann Saile, meaning "Tide Head." The harbor was once an important naval center and was where, on September 21, 1601, a Spanish fleet landed a force of several thousands under Don Juan del Aguila to aid the Irish in their struggle against the English. However, they were overcome at the Battle of Kinsale. A consequence of their defeat was the "Flight of the Earls" from Ireland into foreign service and the eventual submission of the patriot leader O'Neill, after which Kinsale became an English town and Ireland an English dependancy. In 1656, Sir William Penn, at one stage rear admiral of the Irish seas, retired to his Munster Province estate after his release from the Tower of London, taking with him his son, William Penn, the future founder of Pennsylvania. It was while the younger Penn was living in Kinsale that he first heard Thomas Loe, a Quaker itinerant, preach, sowing the seeds of his future radical beliefs.

The origin of kissing the Blarney Stone (right) at Cork's fifteenth-century Blarney Castle (above) to gain eloquence is unknown. However, that "blarney" has become a familiar word is thanks to Queen Elizabeth I of England. She had instructed Cormac MacCarthy, Lord of Blarney, to give up traditional clan methods of electing chiefs and accept land grants from the Crown instead. MacCarthy politicly agreed, but with "fair words and soft speech" procrastinated until the vexed Queen declared: "This is all Blarney: what he says he never means." Ever since, "blarney" has meant the use of charming, flattering, inoffensive words.

Above: the Father Mathew Memorial Church and Parliament Bridge, spanning the south channel of the River Lee. Father Mathew, known as the "Apostle of Temperance," founded the "pledge" movement. Facing page bottom: St. Patrick Street, and (facing page top) the River Lee. The history of Cork (these pages) began when St. Finbarr founded a monastery there in the seventh century. The town survived several Danish raids before England's King Henry II invaded Ireland in 1172 to prevent further Norman proliferation there. In so doing, Henry began the long and bloody association between England and Ireland. St. Colman's Cathedral overlooks Cobh Harbor (overleaf), which lies about fifteen miles away from Cork City. In the old church cemetery lie the graves of several hundred of the 1,198 victims drowned when the liner Lusitania was sunk offshore without warning by a German submarine in 1915.

The mountainous Dingle Peninsula is the most northerly of southwest Ireland's Atlantic promontories and extends about thirty miles westward from the low-lying land around Tralee and Killorglin. The area is associated with St. Brendan; it was from this peninsula that, aged fifty-nine, he began his famous nautical wanderings in a currach, or coracle, made of wood and skins. In this frail vessel he reached the Shetland Islands, Scotland and Iceland. Later, in a new, wooden boat, he reached Newfoundland or Labrador and, from his descriptions of the land and its flora, maybe even Florida. He died in 578, aged about ninety-three.

Above: the view over Smerwick Harbor in County Kerry on the Dingle Peninsula (these pages) looking towards the Three Sisters, and (top) looking towards Kilmalkedar. Smerwick Harbor is infamous for its Dún an Oir, or "Fort of Gold," built in 1579 by a troop of Spaniards. In 1580, its force of 600 Spanish, Italian and Irish soldiers surrendered to the troops of Lord Grey, who then had them massacred, only one man surviving. Among Lord Grey's soldiery was the famous poet, Edmund Spenser.

Coumeenoole Strand, and (overleaf) Doon Point, both on the Dingle Peninsula. About five miles down the coast from Doon Point lies Slea Head, where David Lean filmed Ryan's Daughter. *Its craggy outcrops are said to have been formed by a great volcanic explosion when the lost continent of Atlantis sank into the sea.*

Caherconree Mountain (above), in County Kerry (these pages), is 2,713 feet high and is one of the highest in the Slieve Mish Range. Anascaul (facing page), whose name means "the River of the Hero," lies inland from Dingle Bay. The village was home to Thomas Crean, who went to the Antarctic with Captain Scott in 1910 and was one of the party that found Scott's body. When Crean returned to Anascaul he opened a pub called the "South Pole Inn."

The Gallerus Oratory (above), near Ballyferriter, is one of the oldest unmortared-stone Christian churches to be found anywhere. This tiny structure, only fifteen by ten feet with walls three feet thick, is still watertight after over 1,200 years. The unmortared beehive huts (facing page), or clocháns, found on the Dingle Peninsula (these pages) were probably used as cells by ascetic monks. Some have been radio-carbon dated to several centuries before the sixth century – previously their earliest approximated date.

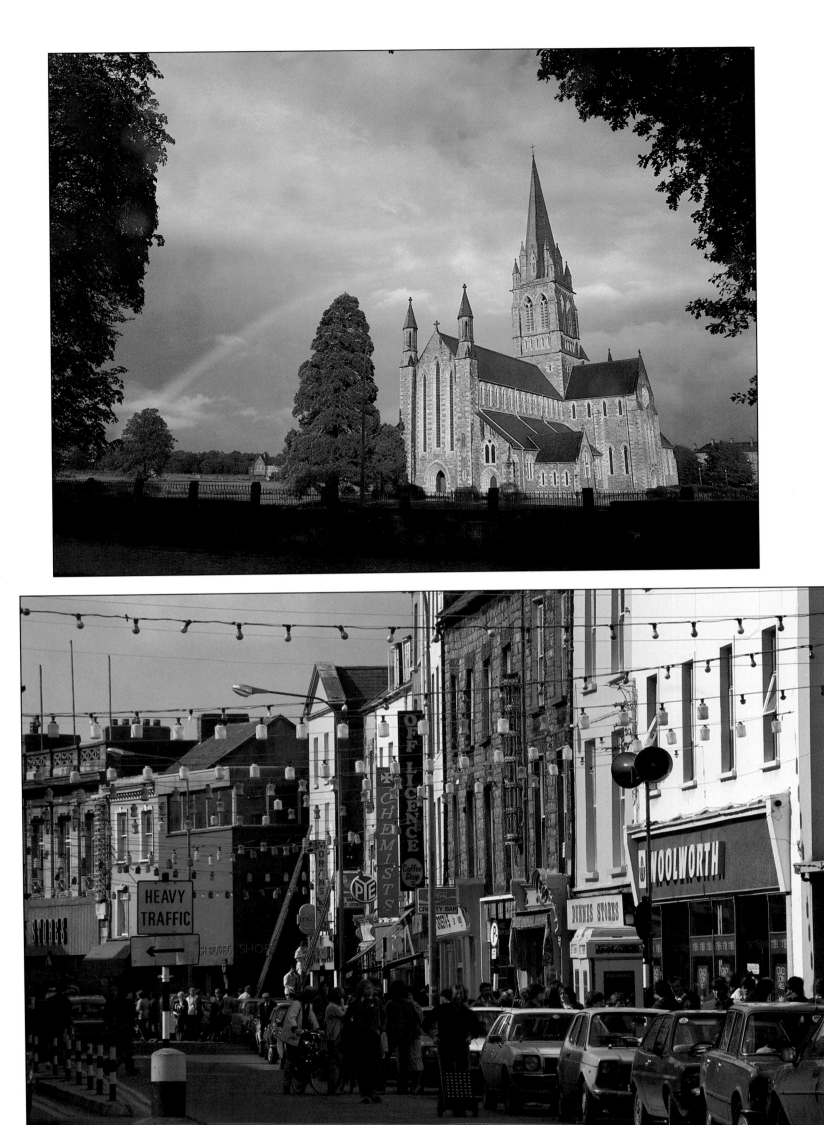

Above: Castle Street, Tralee, (top) St. Mary's Cathedral, Killarney, and (facing page) Main Street, Dingle, County Kerry (these pages). Dingle people are said to be darker than other Irish people because of their early intermarriage with Spanish traders. It is also said that the Scythian Fenius Farsa, having refused to help persecute Egyptian Jews, eventually fled to the Dingle Peninsula with his daughter Scota, son-in-law Milesius and grandson Goidel, establishing the race variously called Fenians, Scots, Milesians and Goidels – or Gaels.

Lakeland (left and overleaf) near Killarney, County Kerry, draws many visitors. The lake complex of Killarney was scooped out of the limestone valleys of the Old Red Sandstone Mountains by glacial action.

These pages: the Owenreagh River near Moll's Gap, County Kerry.

Muckross House near Killarney was presented to the people of Ireland in 1932, together with its 10,000-acre estate, by its American owner, Mr. William Bowers Bourn. On its presentation, Mr. Bourn's son-in-law, Senator Arthur Vincent, said: "I hope that Muckross will be made a real garden of friendship, and that it will be the greatest playground in the world – there is not another in the world like it, and I know them all."

Tudor-style Muckross House (these pages) was built in 1843 on the site of a house in which Rudolph Erich Raspe, who wrote The Adventures of Baron Munchausen, *once lived. The house is now run as a museum where traditional weaving methods (facing page top) may still be seen in practise. Overleaf: the ruins of Muckross Abbey, near Killarney, founded by Donal MacCarthy Mor and occupied by Franciscans in 1448. It was raided in 1589 by Elizabethan soldiery and finally ruined in 1652 by Cromwellians.*

The Irish name for the Cliffs of Moher, Aillte an Mhothair, *means the "Cliffs of Ruin." These cliffs, in County Clare, are formed from horizontal layers of flagstone and are relentlessly pounded by the Atlantic. They extend for five miles and have a 700-foot drop in places. The flagstone is quarried locally and marketed as Liscannor slate, some of which was incorporated into the steps of Westminster Cathedral, London. In his book* The Way That I Went, *Robert Lloyd Praeger said of the cliffs: "They are too steep to support plant life, and provide few ledges whereon seabirds can nest or rest, which gives them a grim and savage look."*

Left: Kingstown Bay, west of Clifden, near Connemara, and (top left) the Twelve Bens beyond Lake Maumeen, County Galway, among which are the conical peaks of Benbaun, which is the highest, Bencorr and Bencollaghduff – all of them over 2,000 feet high. Above: Roundstone Harbor, its name an English corruption of Cloc an Ron, *meaning "Rock of the Seal," lies at the foot of Errisbeg Mountain in Connemara, County Galway.*

Kingstown Bay, near Connemara. Lough Corrib (overleaf), near Cornamona, is bordered to the north by Joyce's Country, named for a Welsh family that settled in the region in the thirteenth century. Lough Corrib is Ireland's second-largest lake and is linked to Lough Mask by underground streams.

The southern shore of Ballynahinch Lough (facing page), in Connemara, County Galway, was home to the renowned duelist, "Hair-trigger Dick," or Richard Martin (1754-1834), who eventually became a founder of the Royal Society for the Prevention of Cruelty to Animals. Above: Roundstone, overlooking Ballinakill Bay, and (top) countryside near Leenane, both in County Galway.

The Dawros River, and (overleaf) the rushing waters of the Owenriff River, both in County Galway.

Killary Harbor, in County Mayo, is Ireland's only fjord. It is so deep and sheltered that it could accommodate the entire navy of any world power. Indeed, its eight-mile-long inlet was, at one time, a naval station.

Above: Asleagh Falls near Leenane. The abbey (top) at Cong, County Mayo, was founded for the Order of St. Augustine in the twelfth century by the last King of Ireland, Roderick O'Connor, who died here in 1198. Facing page: Downpatrick Head, County Mayo. Croagh Patrick (overleaf), overlooking Clew Bay in County Mayo, is Ireland's holy mountain. Here, in A.D. 441, Saint Patrick is said to have spent the forty days of Lent fasting and praying for the Irish. His statue stands at the foot of the mountain.

Ashford Castle (these pages), in Cong, County Mayo, is now a hotel but was, until 1939, the country home of the Guinness family. Its history goes back to 1228, when the Norman family of De Burgo came to the west of Ireland and built a castle at Cong, which they held until the forces of Queen Elizabeth I of England seized it and built a fortress on its site. The present castle dates from 1715, but was considerably altered in 1852. The surrounding villages and scenery will be familiar to all those who have seen the movie The Quiet Man, *which was filmed in the area.*

Westport Bay lies on the southeastern corner of Clew Bay, near Murrisk, in County Mayo. In 1842, William Makepeace Thakeray described it as the "most beautiful [bay] in the world." Lough Conn (overleaf), near Crossmolina in County Mayo, is linked to Lough Cullin by a short channel, spanned by the Pontoon Bridge. The lough is famous for its fishing and, in 1920, a monster pike weighing fifty-three pounds was caught in its waters.

The Donegal coast, in the northwest of Ireland, is hemmed with long sandy beaches.

Above: Carrick-a-rede, meaning "the passage of the salmon," near Ballintoy, County Antrim, and (facing page) White Rocks, County Antrim, carpeted with sea pinks. Belfast's Renaissance-style City Hall (overleaf), designed by Bramwell Thomas, was completed by 1906. Following page: a lone fishing boat on the northwest coast.

INDEX